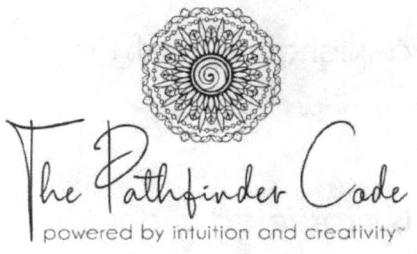

"Mindset Magic"
Coloring Book

BY
LILY NAVA-NICHOLSON

Copyright© 2020 by Lily Nava-Nicholson and The Pathfinder Code®

All rights reserved. This book is protected under the copyright laws of the United States of America. No part of this publication may be reproduced, distributed, or transmitted in any form or by any means, including photocopying, recording or other electronic or mechanical methods without the prior written permission from the author.

For permissions, please contact the author.

Cover Design: Lily Nava-Nicholson

Interior: Lily Nava-Nicholson

Paperback ISBN: 9798552600441

Published by: Lily Nava-Nicholson / The Pathfinder Code®

www.lilynavagallery.com

www.thepathfindercode.com

Hello Beautiful Soul!

You will find all of the images in this MINDSET MAGIC COLORING BOOK at www.lilynavagallery.com

(1) Getting started! Every page in the coloring book has the <u>title</u> of the original painting. Pick one....

(2) Next, go to my art website at the url provided to match it up with the image and title you are coloring in the book! Note-some of the coloring pages are for you to use your imagination and deep dive!

(3) Next, create <u>your own version of my painting</u> with the colors that both enchant and speak to you!

(4) Next, Join my <u>Pathfinder Code® Group on Facebook</u>.

THIS GROUP IS WHERE YOU WILL <u>SHARE YOUR COLORING BOOK CREATION.</u>

(5) Once you share your photo <u>you will be entered in a drawing for a limited edition print</u> of that image or another one from my private collection!

With Love & Gratitude for you... *Lily Nava-Nicholson*

ABOUT LILY: Hello! I am Lily Nava-Nicholson. I am a self-taught visionary artist, Author and Intuitive Life & Success Coach.. My paintings bring to life the essence of the "in between" energy and visions I interpret living in what I believe to be a multidimensional universe.

I paint from a soul level channeling from flow. My paintings are portals that transport viewers to enchanted realms that whisper sacred words of wisdom meant just for them.

Painting and empowering others are my passions and what led me to create <u>The Pathfinder Code®: Powered by Intuition and Creativity</u>

My artistic and coaching services also branch out to individuals and entrepreneurs/businesses in the form:

Private Individual or Group Coaching. Employee engagement through team mindset trainings.

Virtual consults to explore transforming clients' spaces through the placement of my orignal inspirational art as a focal point.

 I am also passionate in my support of meaningful causes which have a common theme to support planetary sustainability, world peace and our people.

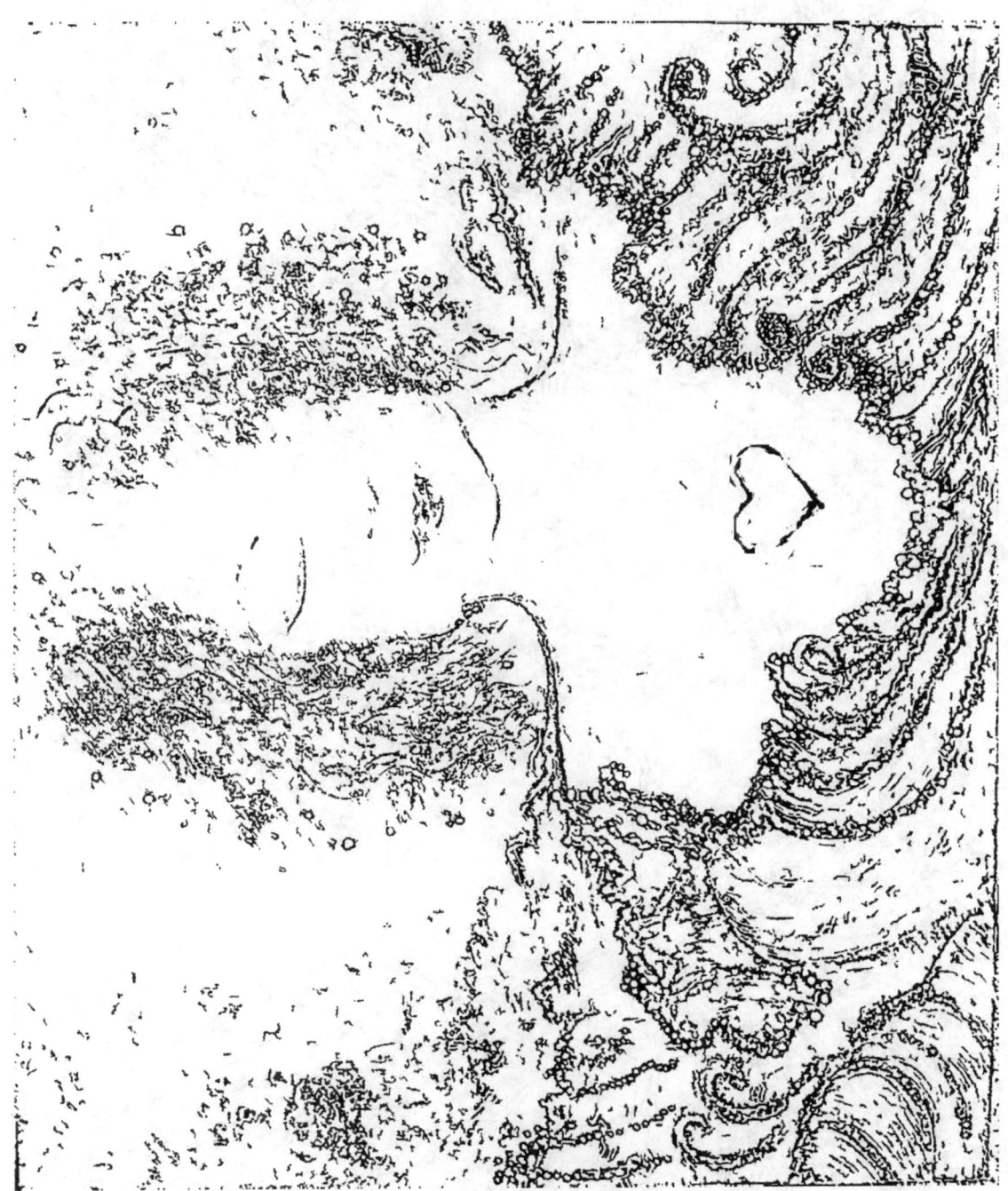

MERMAID MEDITATION

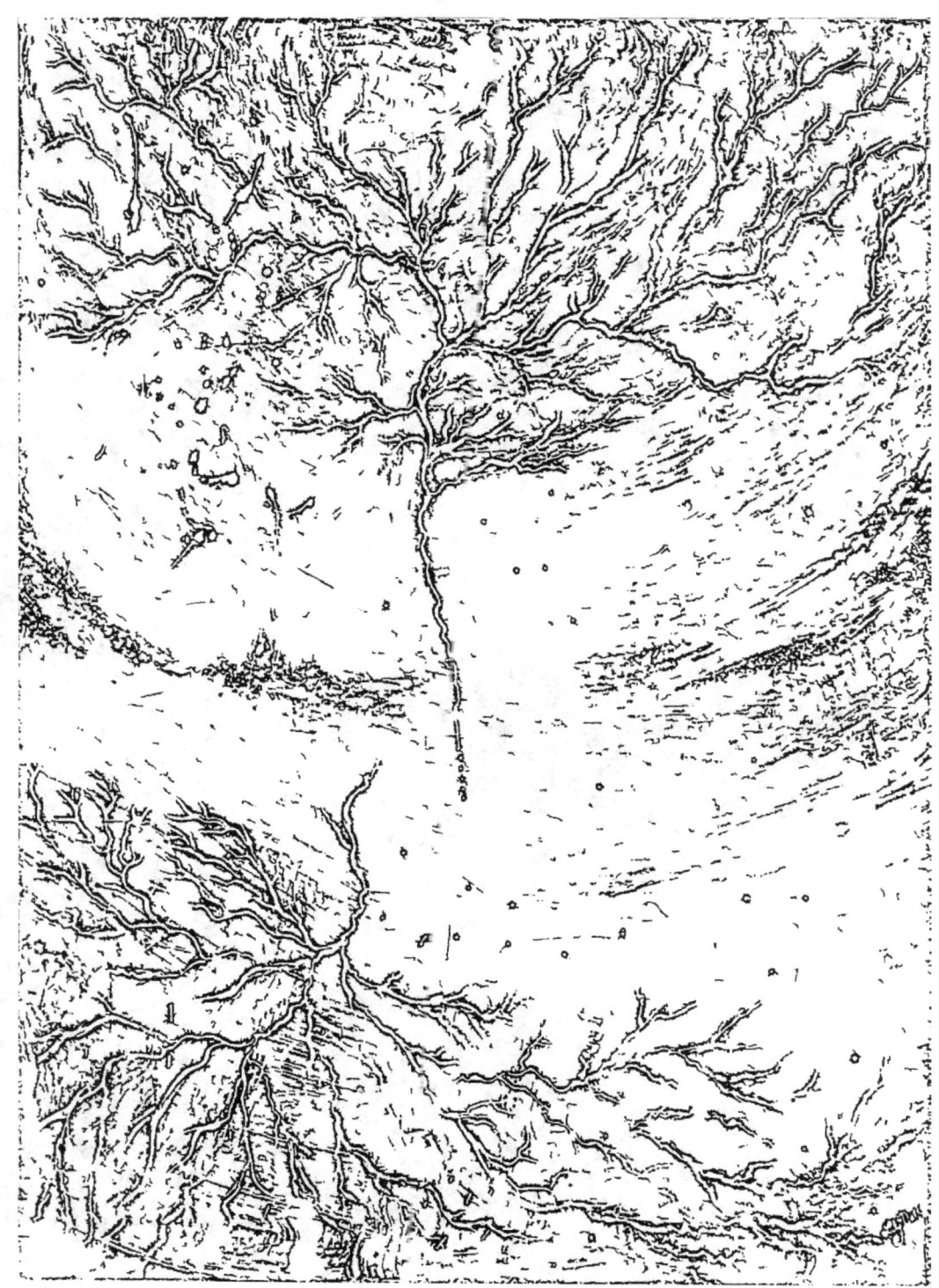

ALPHA & OMEGA

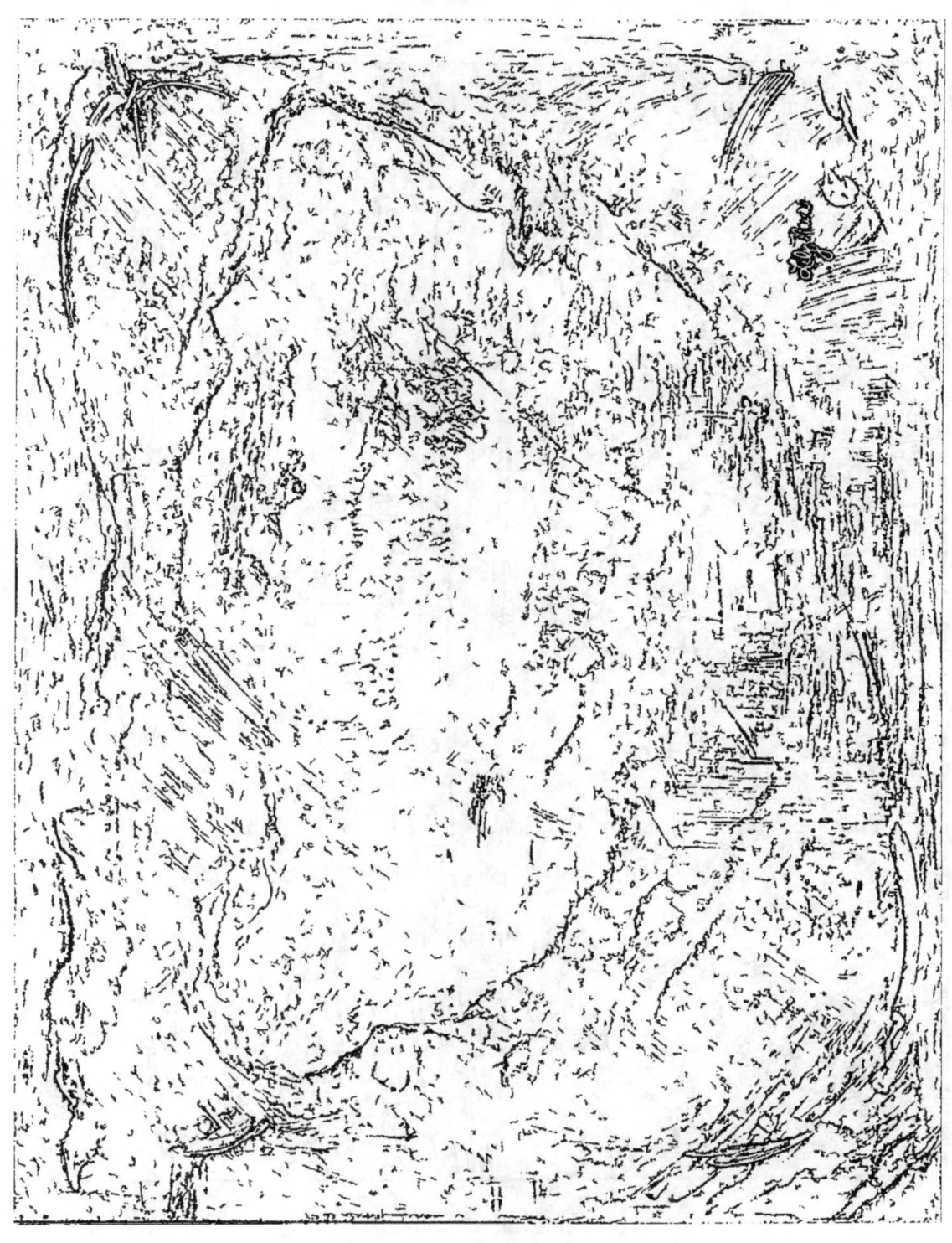

ANCIENT LIGHT

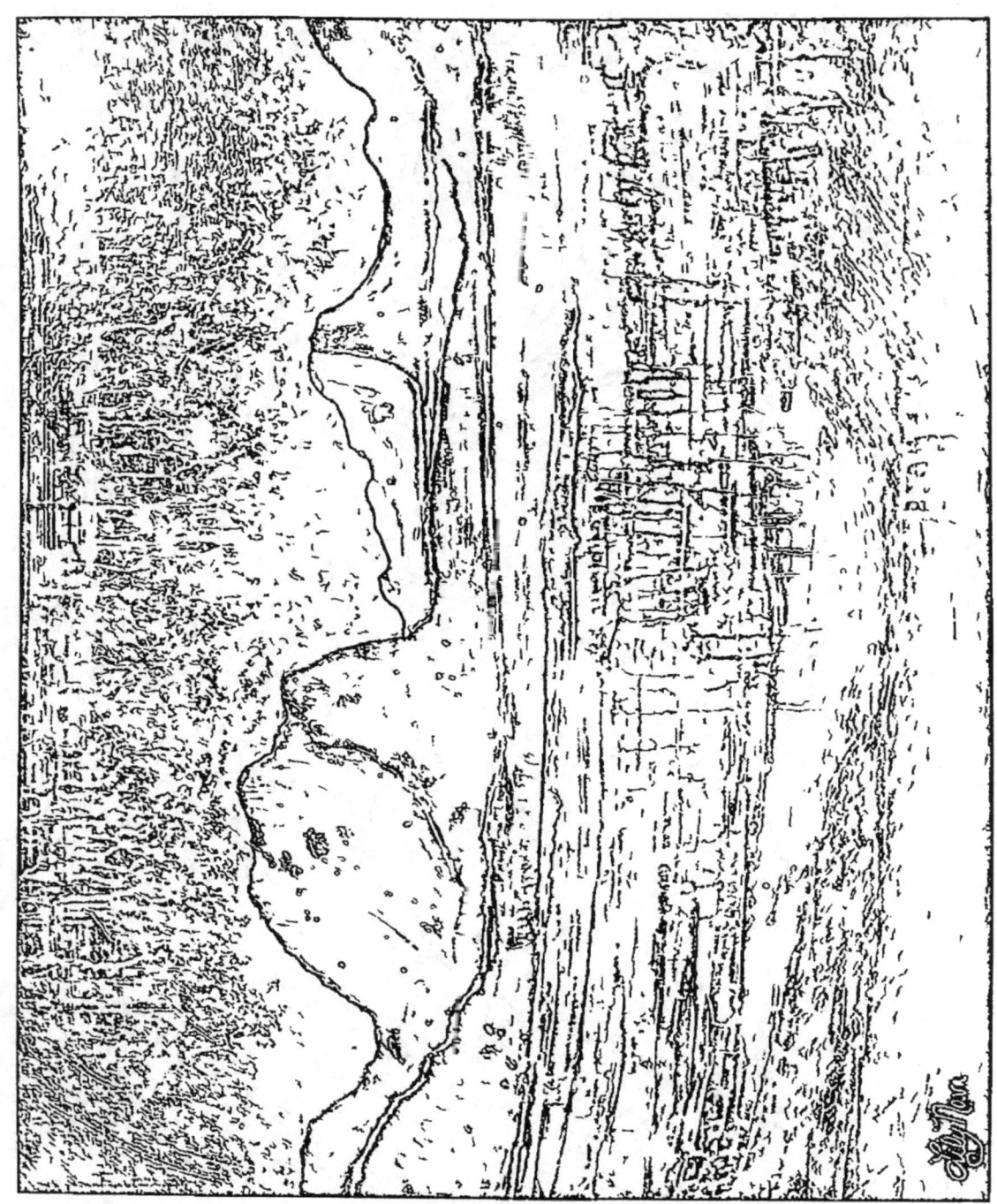

ANCIENT RAIN

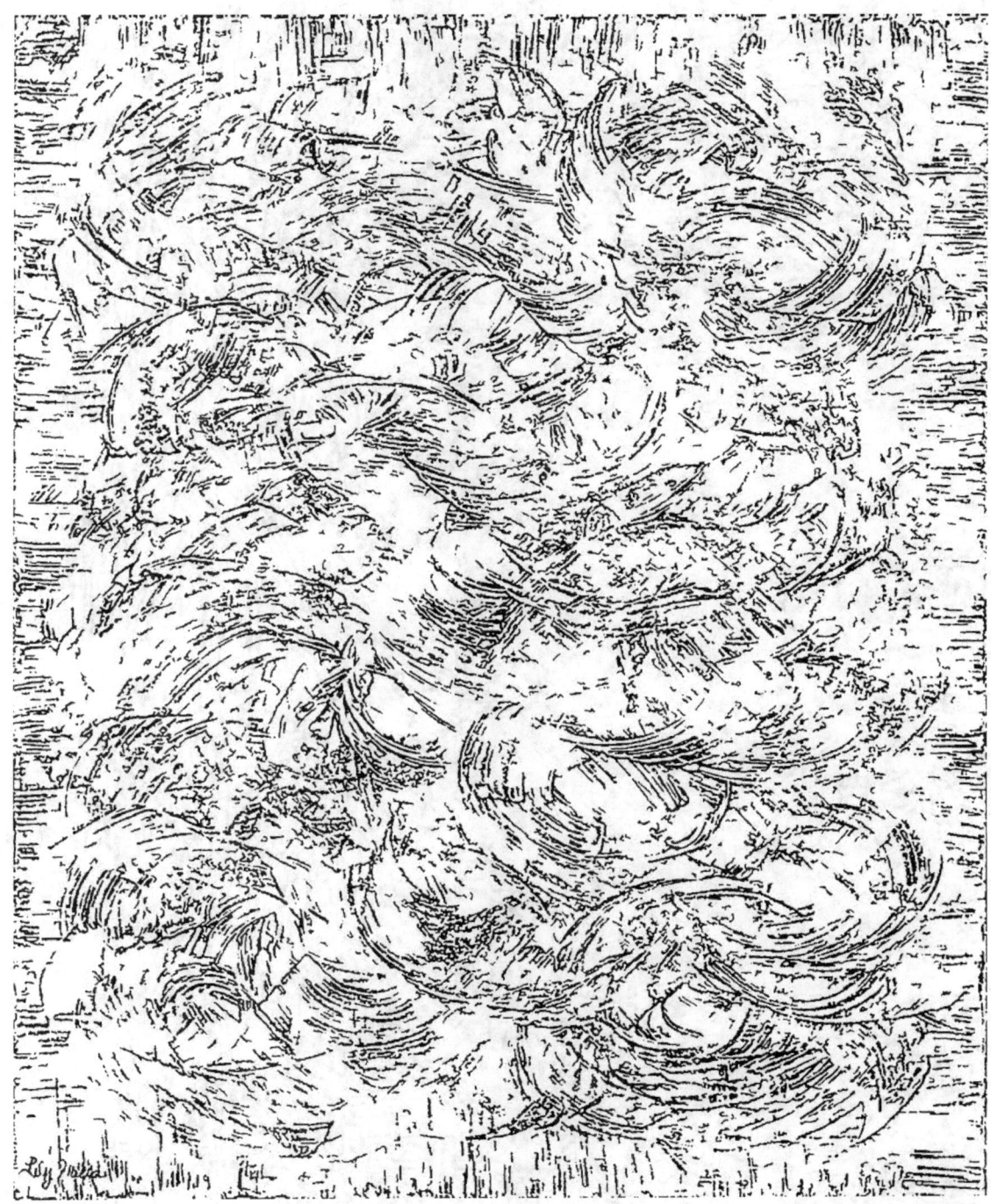

ARTISTS' CHALLENGE

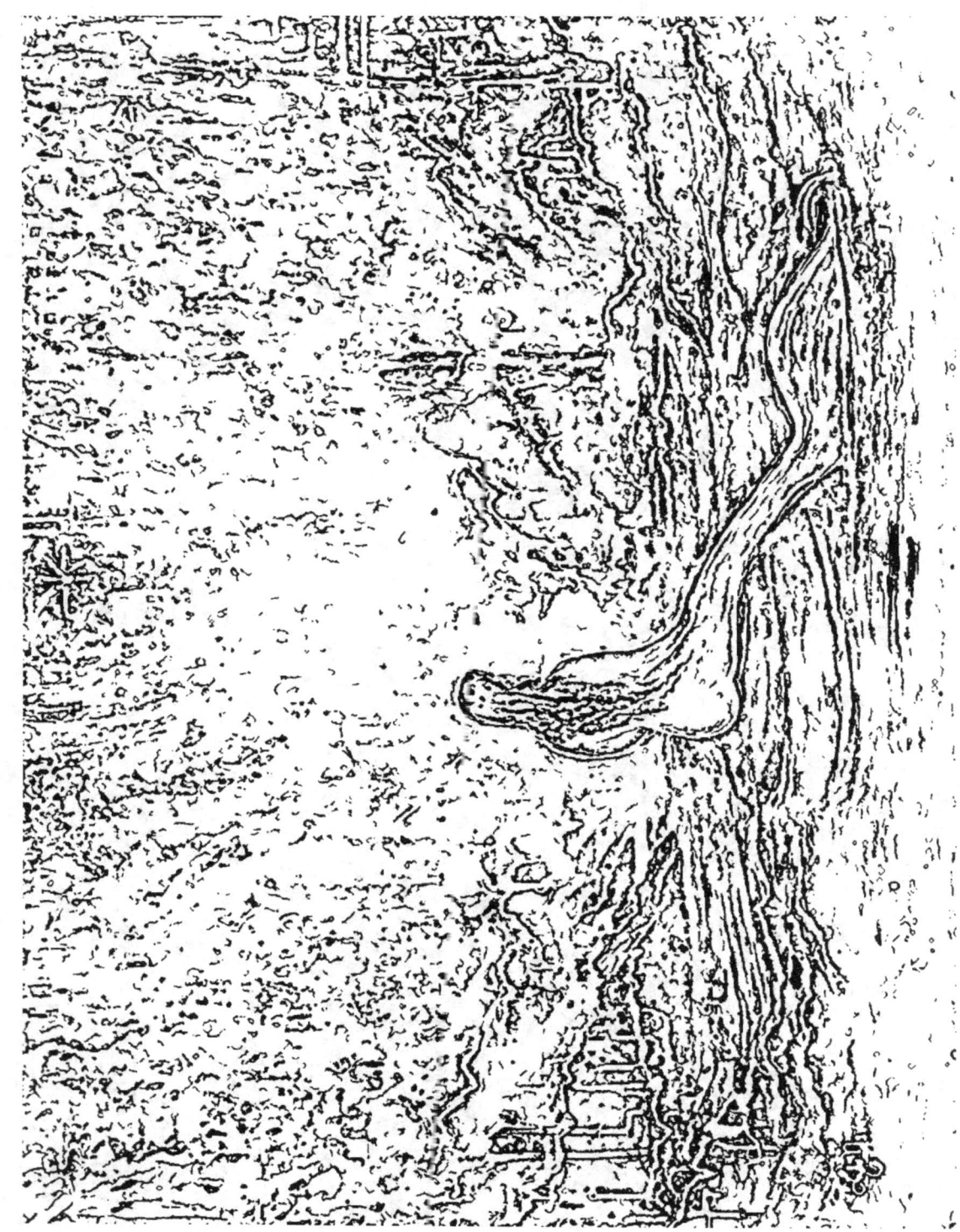

ATLANTIAN VISION

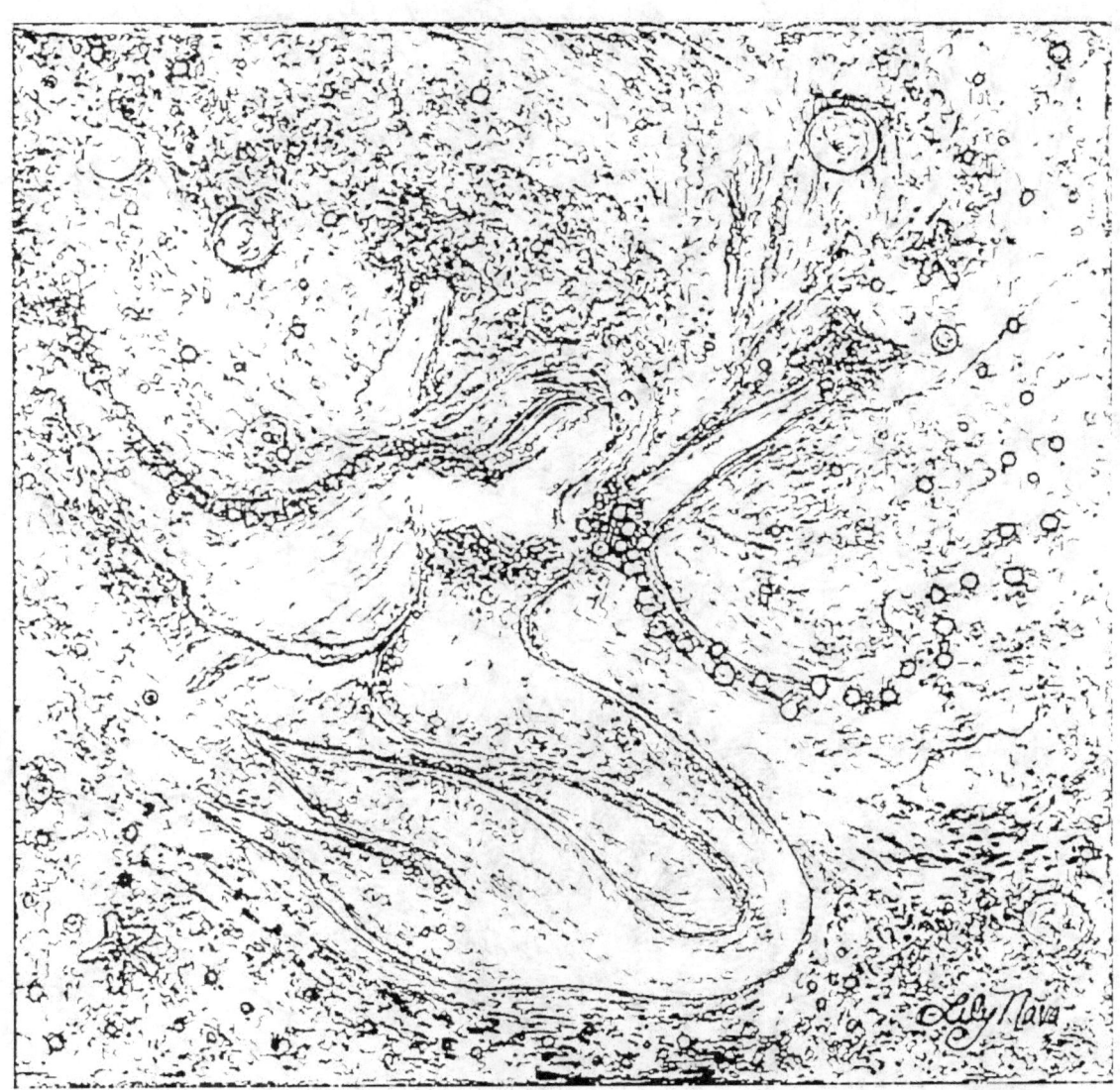

BLISS

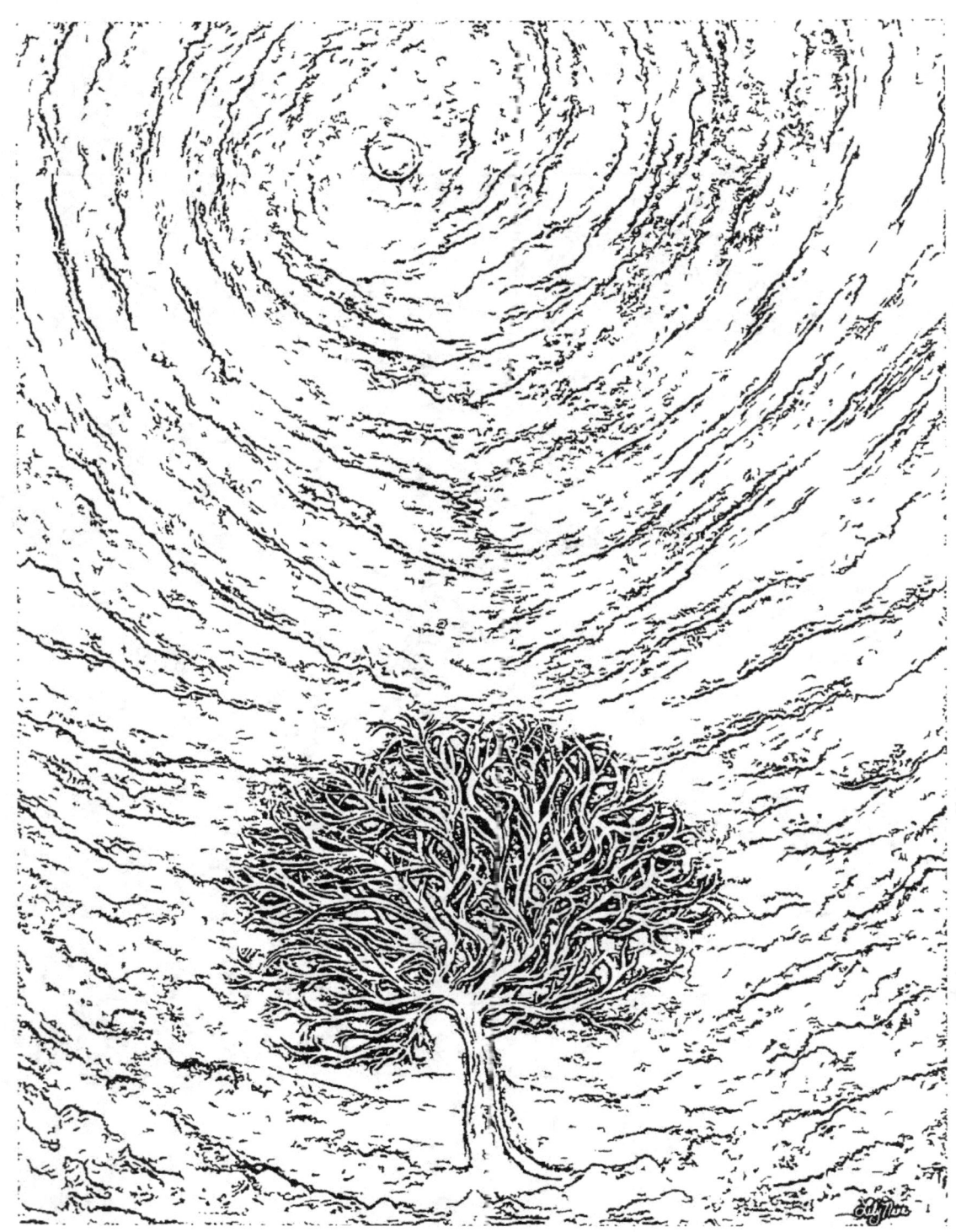

EARTH SONG

TOP OF IMAGE

EDGE OF ETERNITY

TOP OF IMAGE

ENCHANTED FOREST

TOP OF IMAGE

ENCHANTED REALM

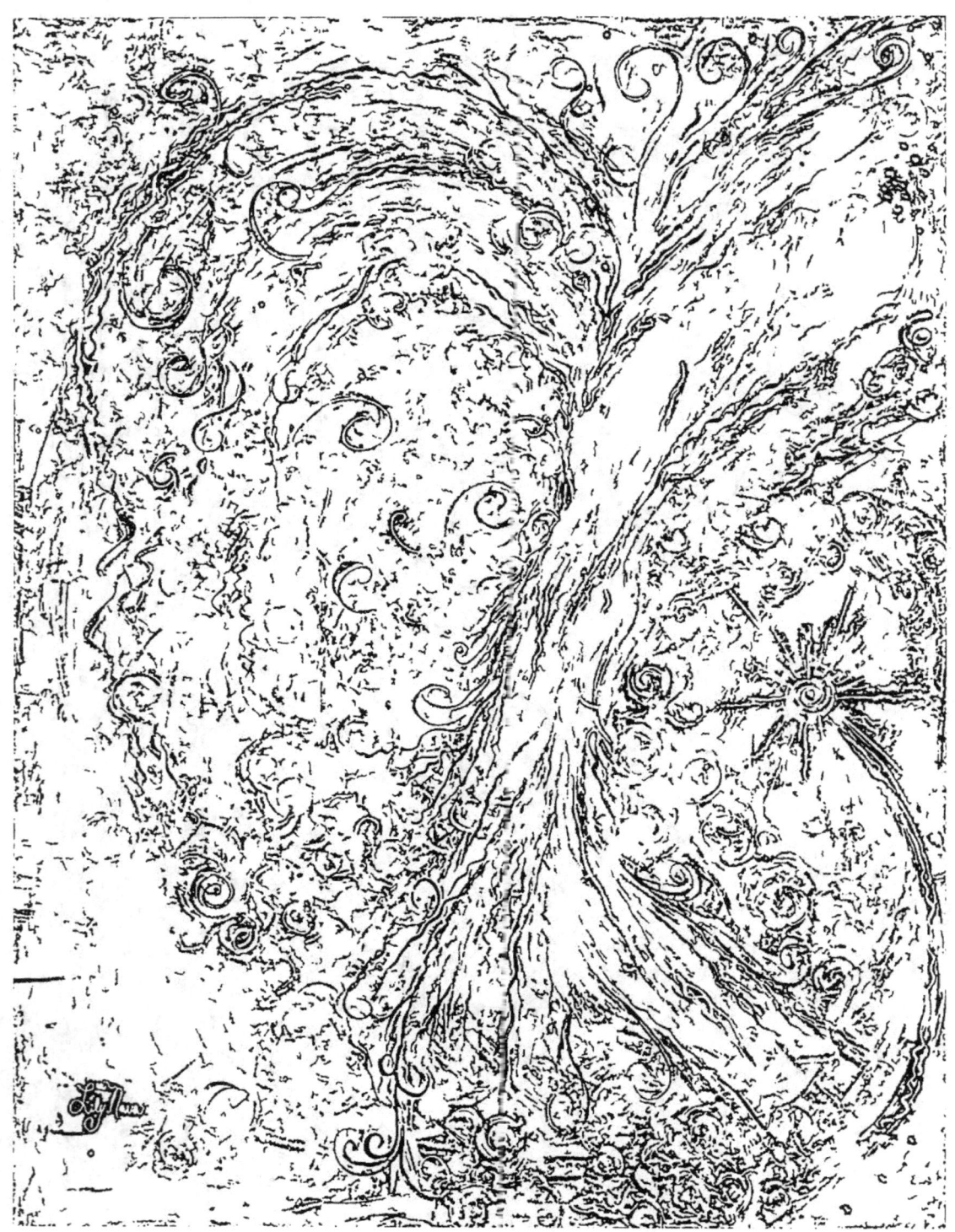
FAIRIES PARADISE

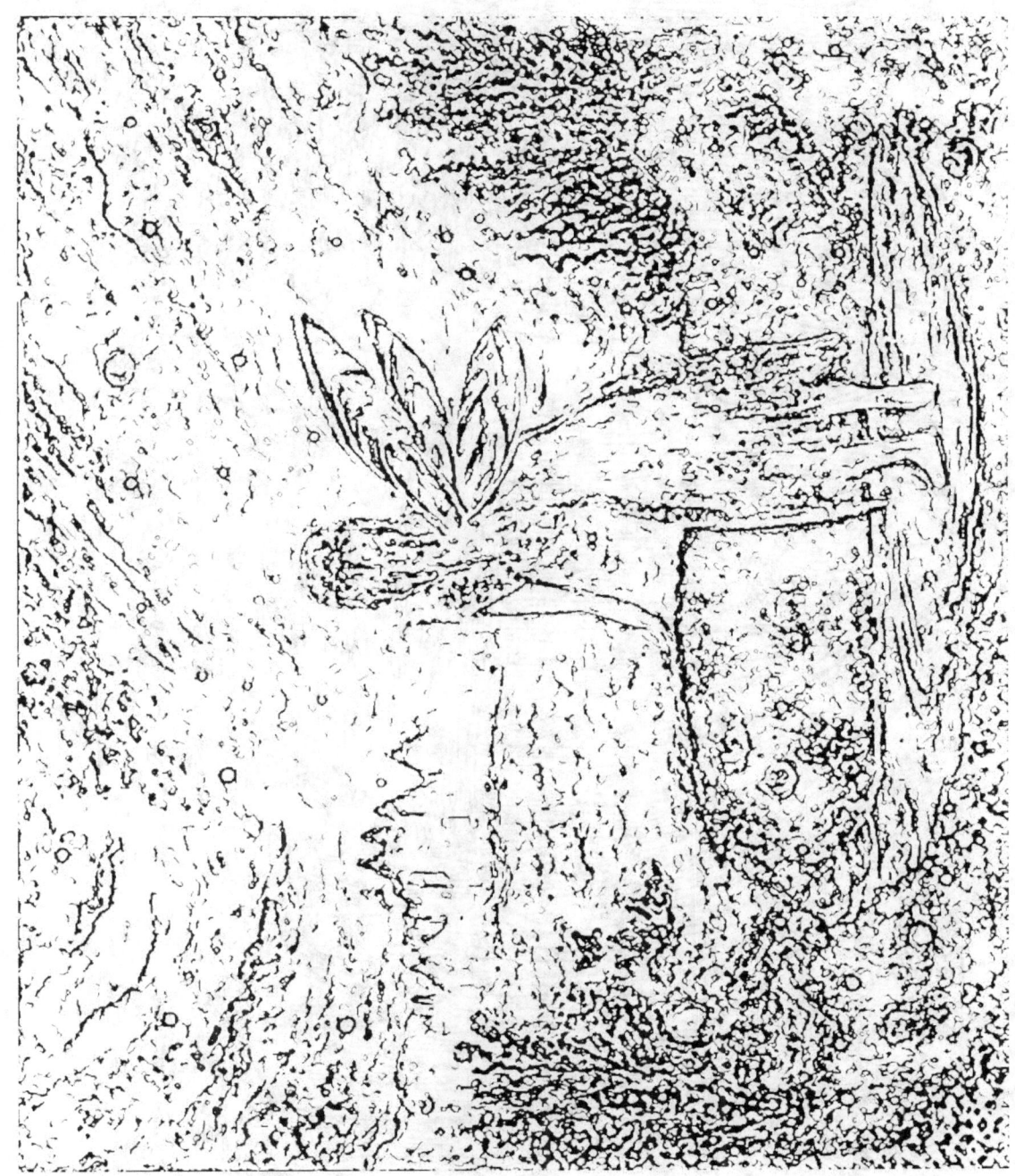

FAIRYTALE

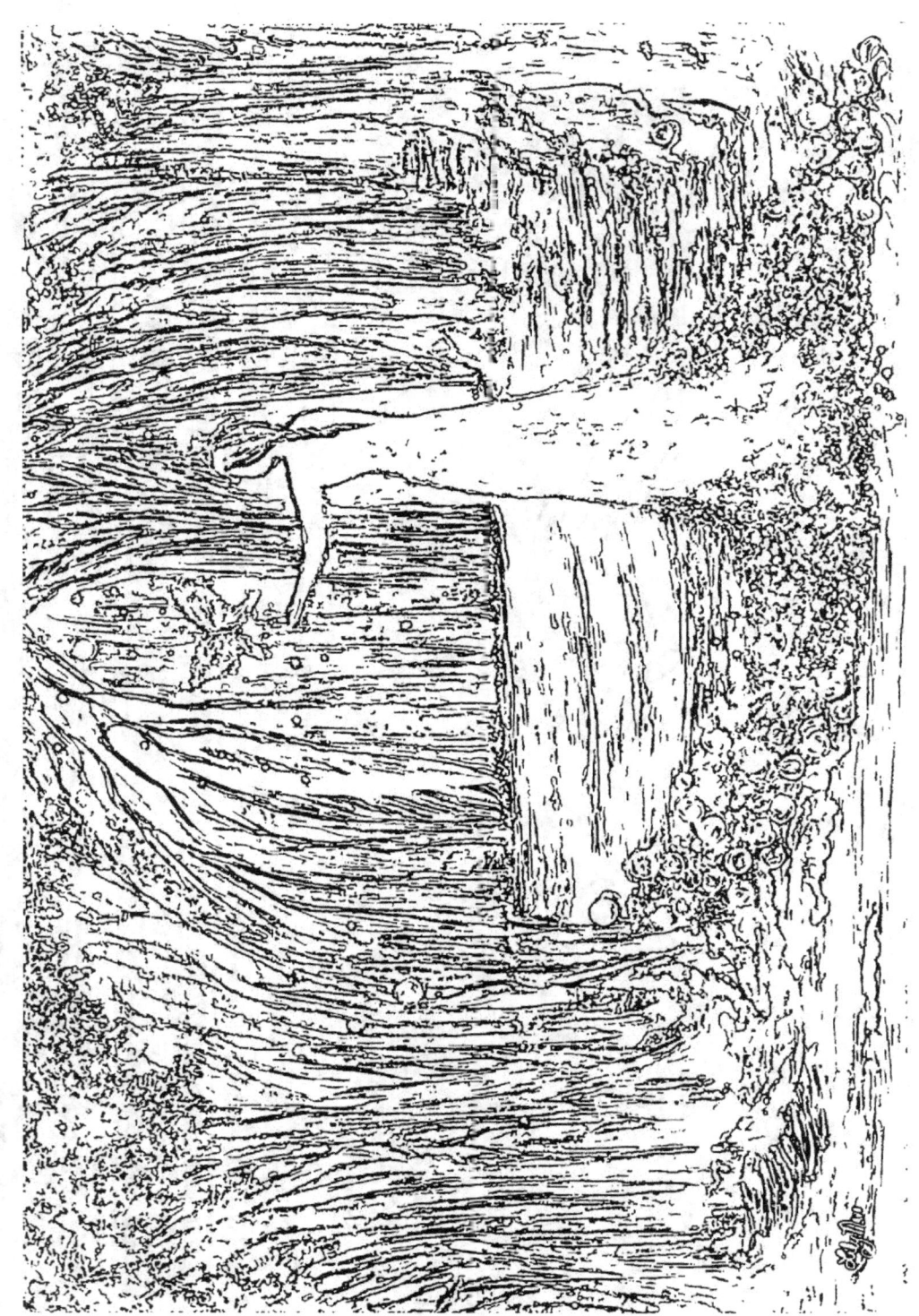
GAIA, GODDESS OF EARTH

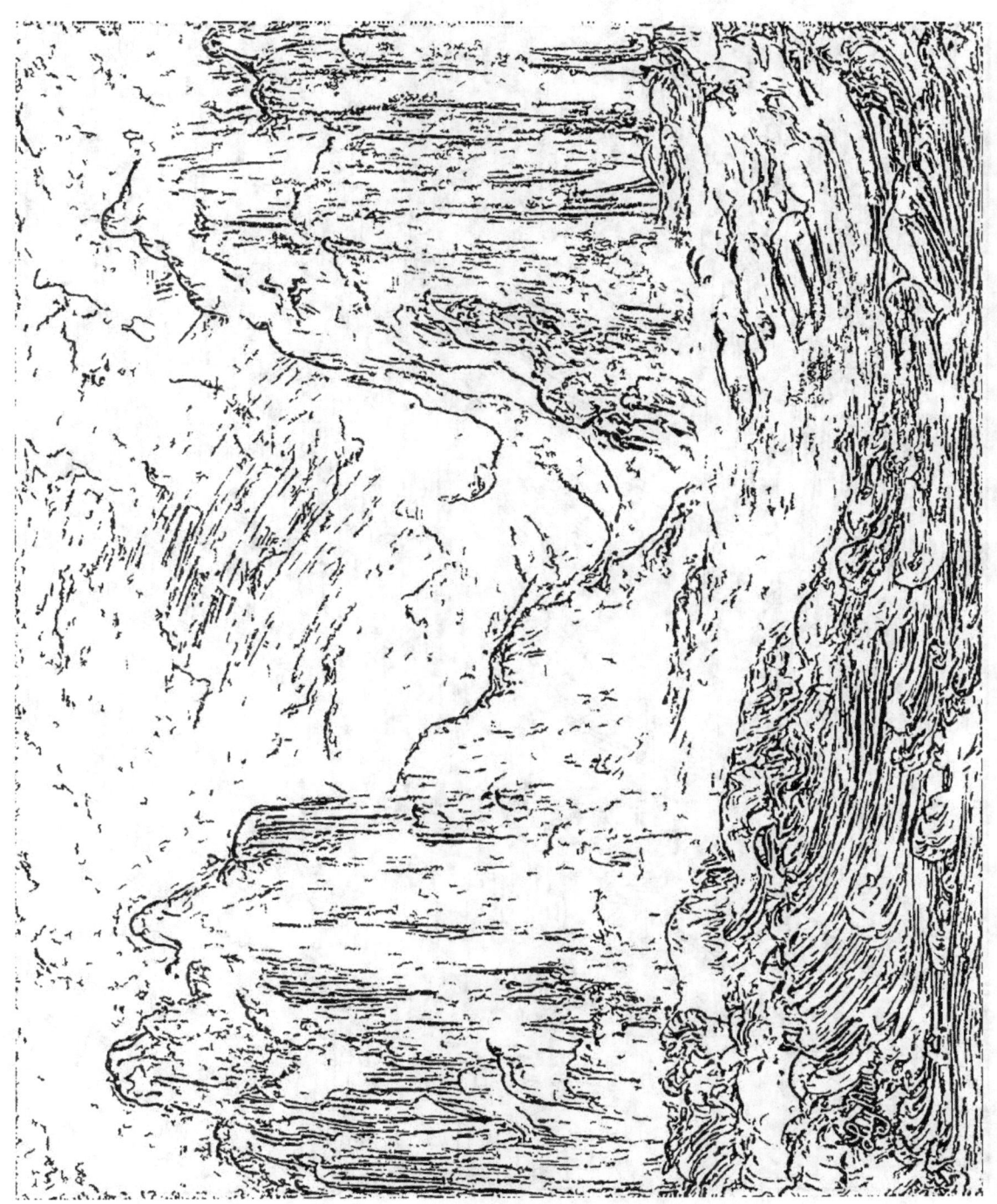

HEAVEN, EARTH, SEDONA

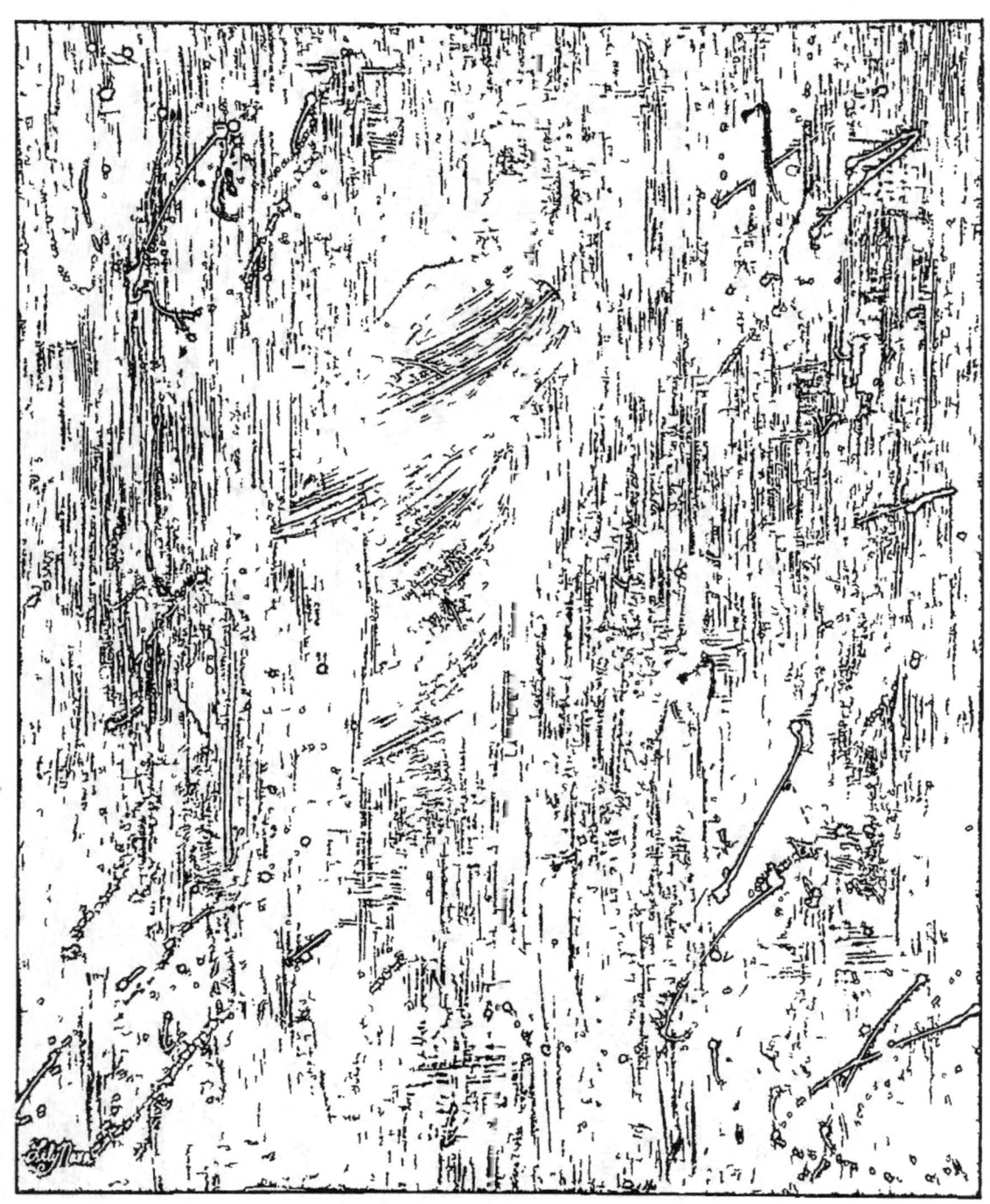

ILLLMINATA I

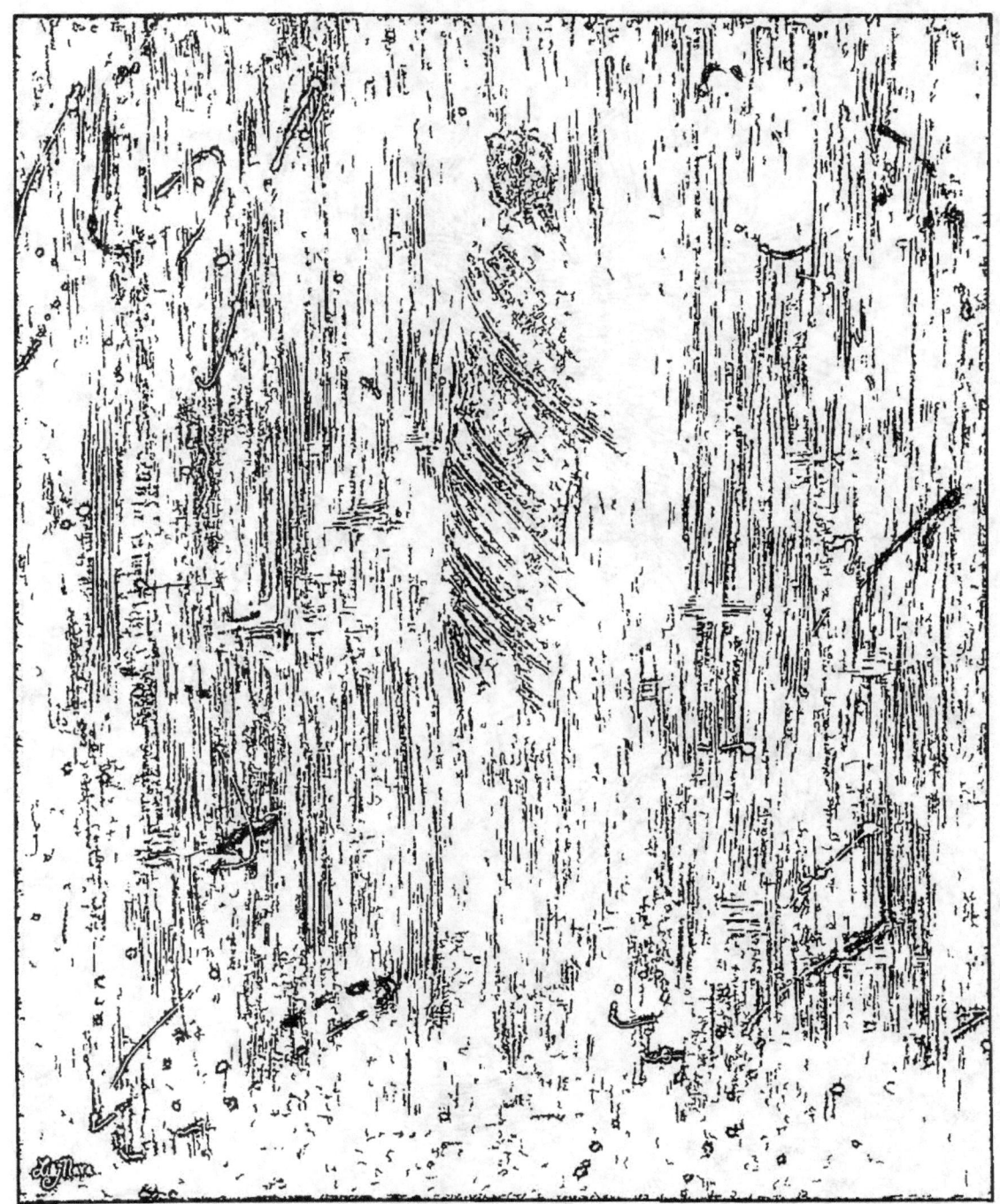

ILLUMINATA II

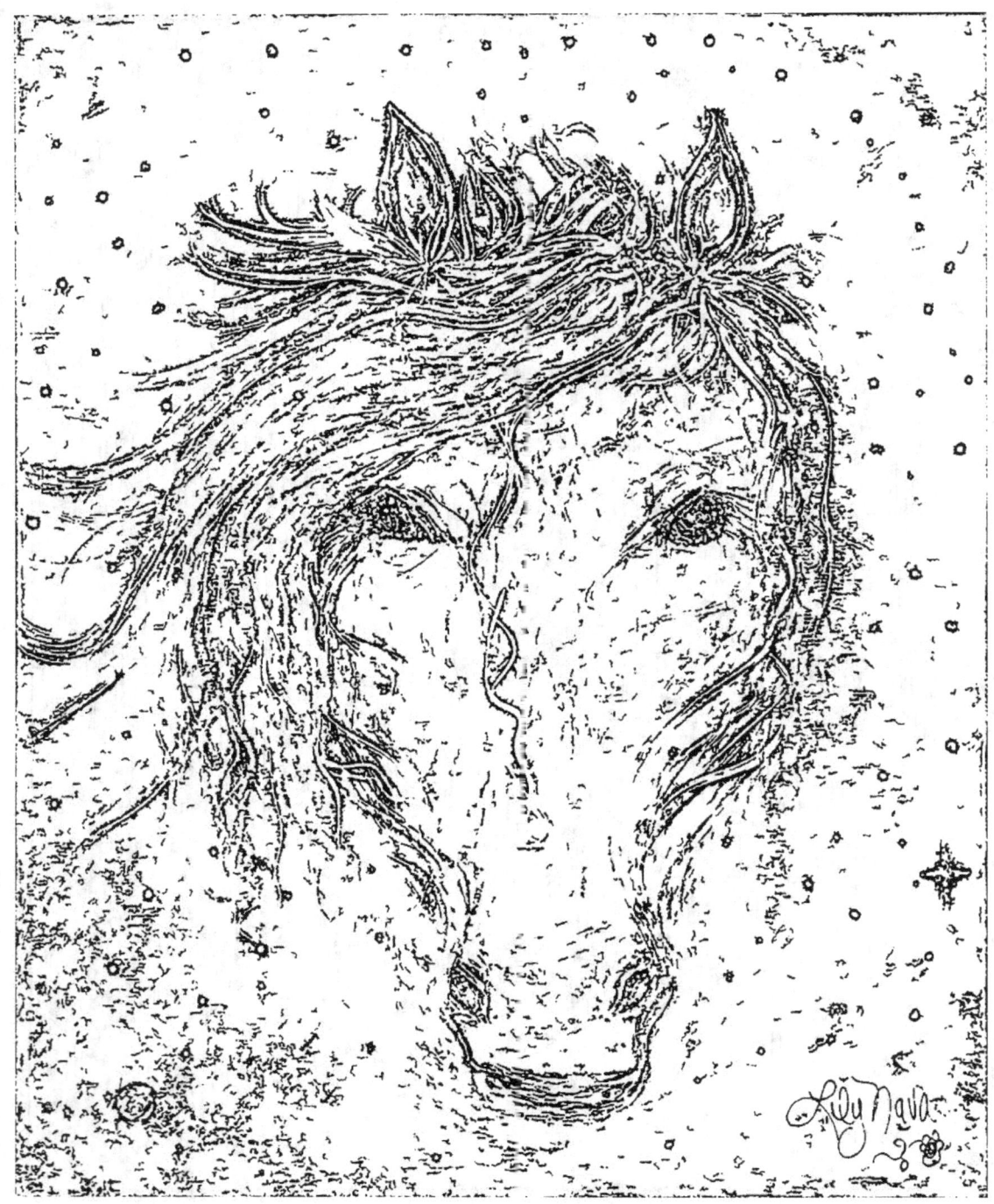

INDIGO STAR

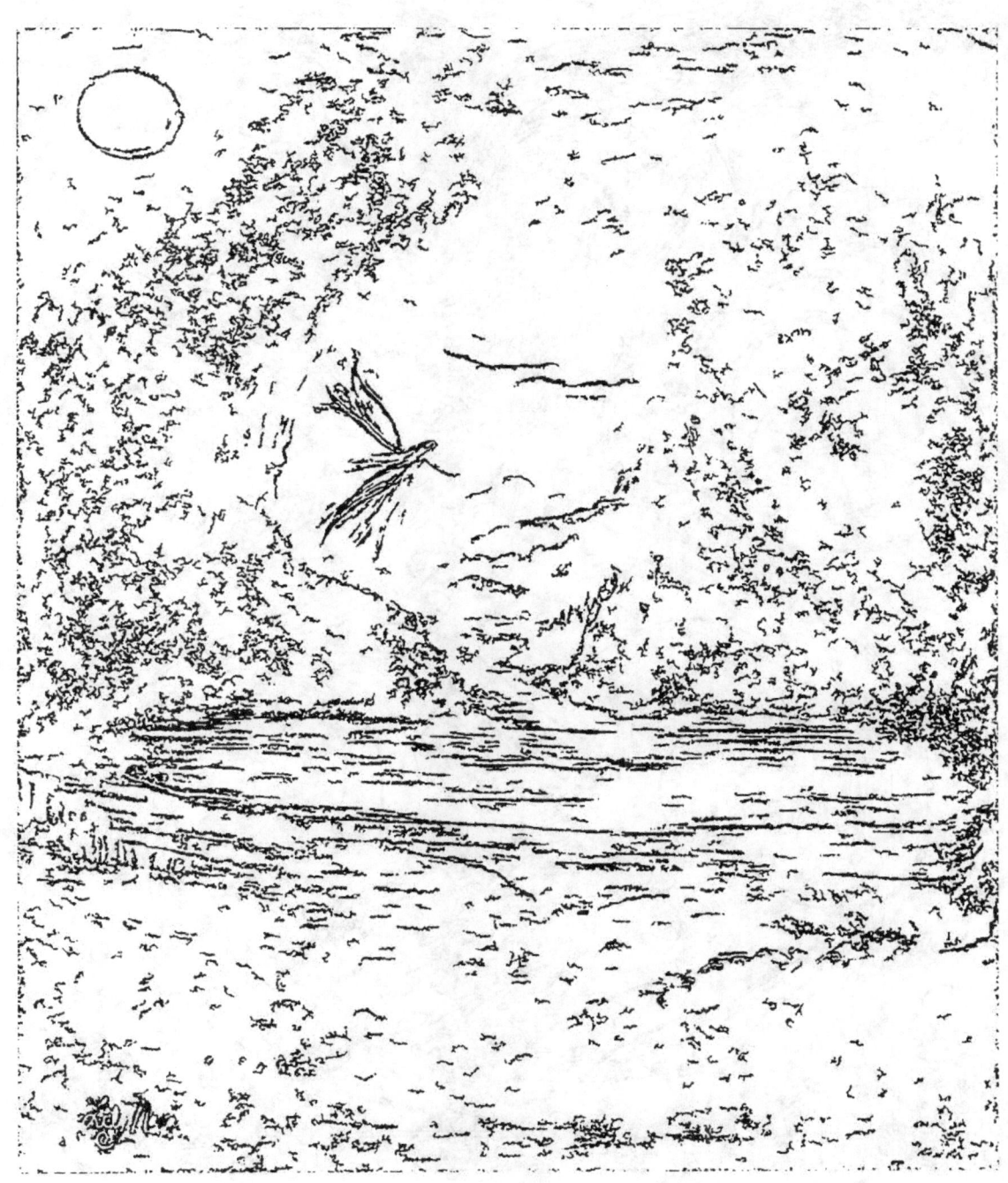

JOURNEY

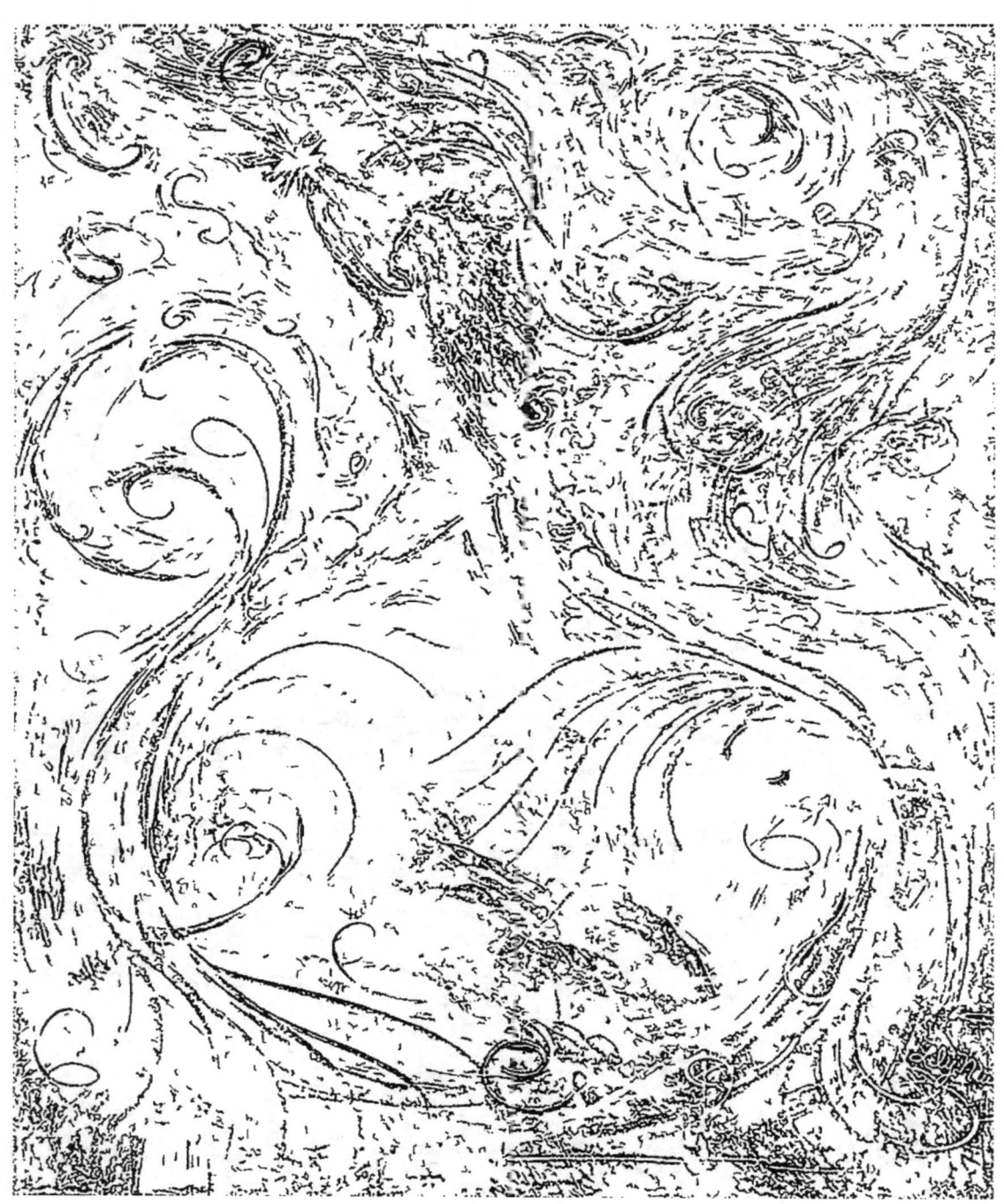

LIGHTBEARER'S GIFT

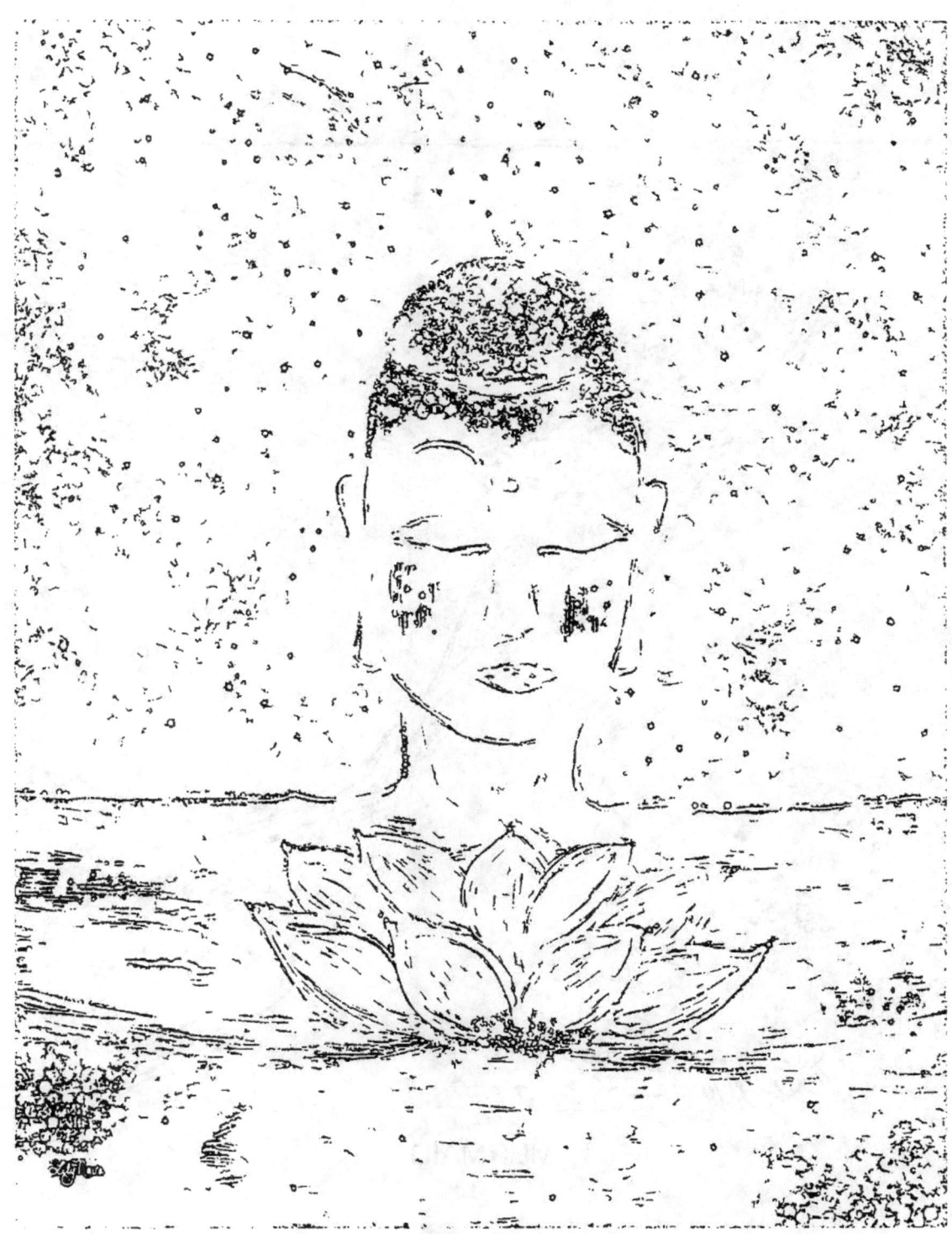

LOTUS DREAM

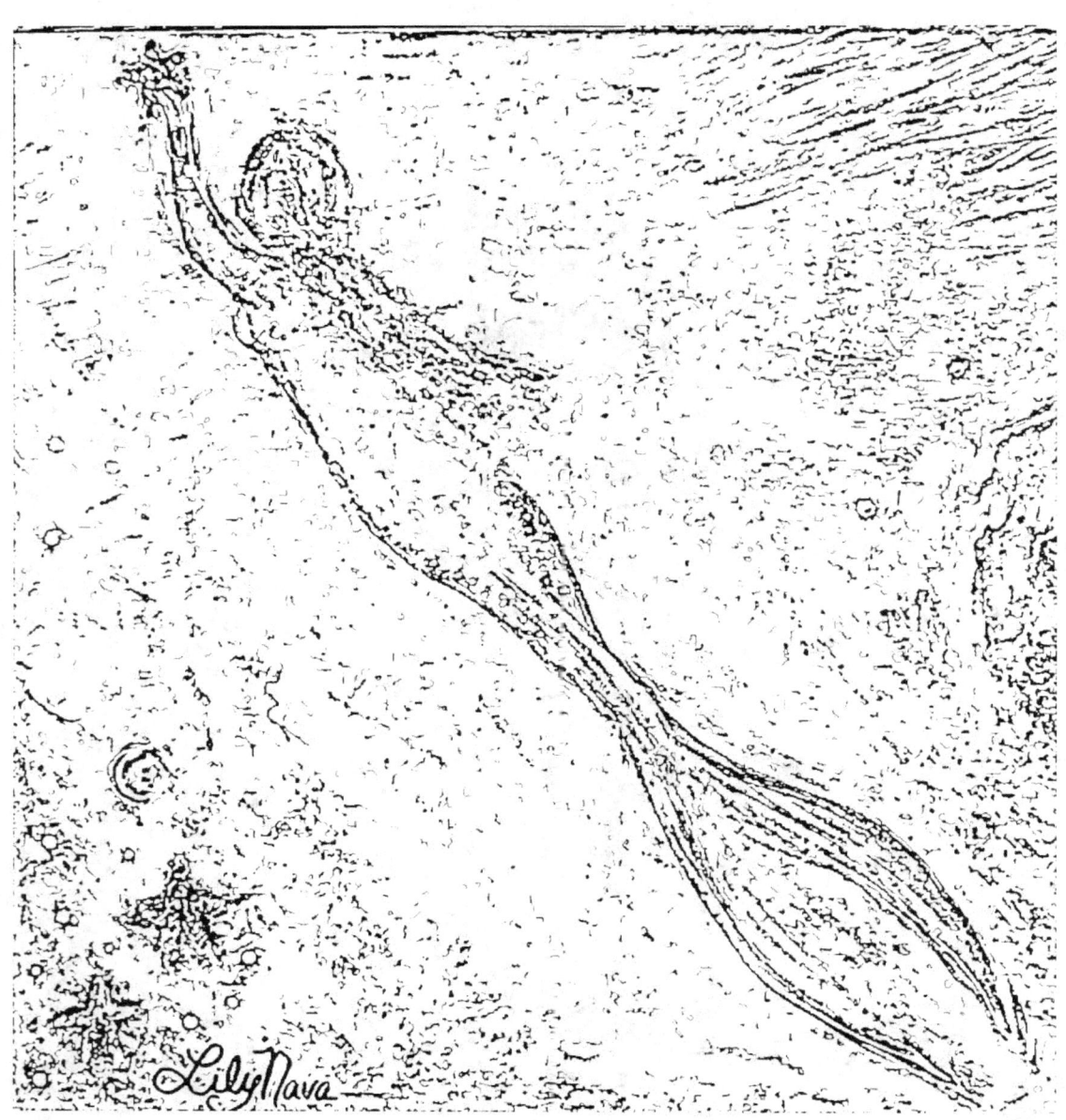

MERMAID

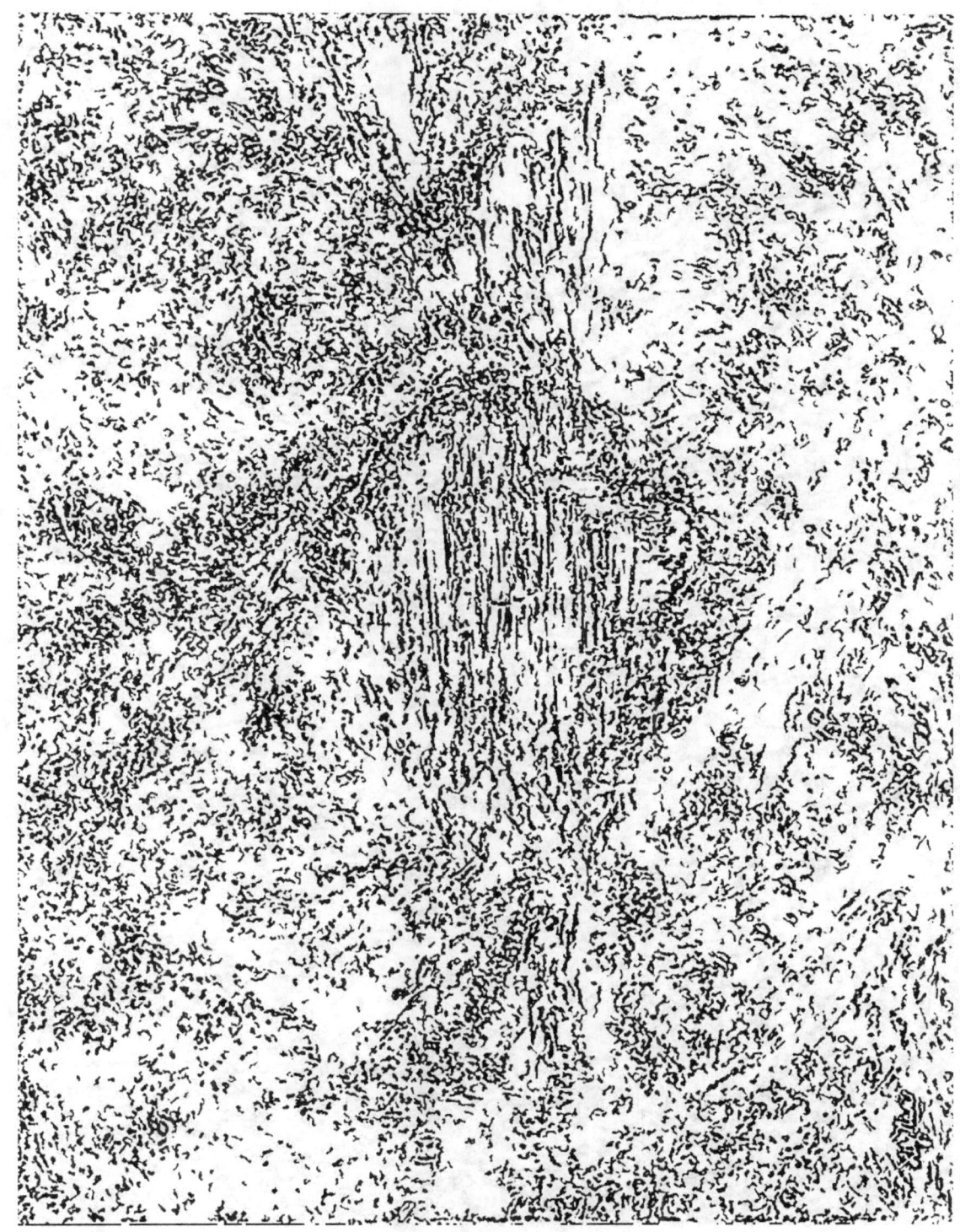

MYSTIC FOREST

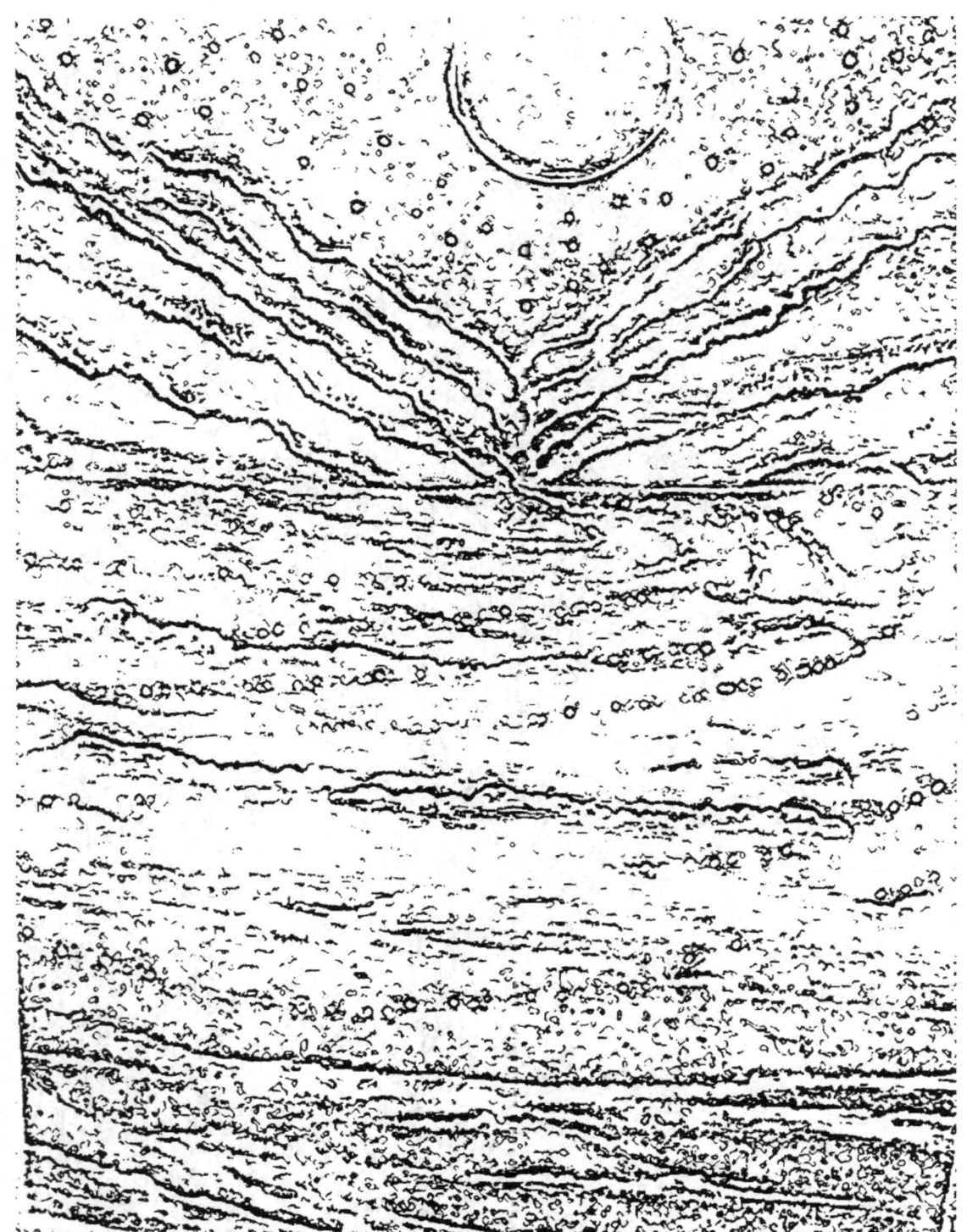

NEW EARTH

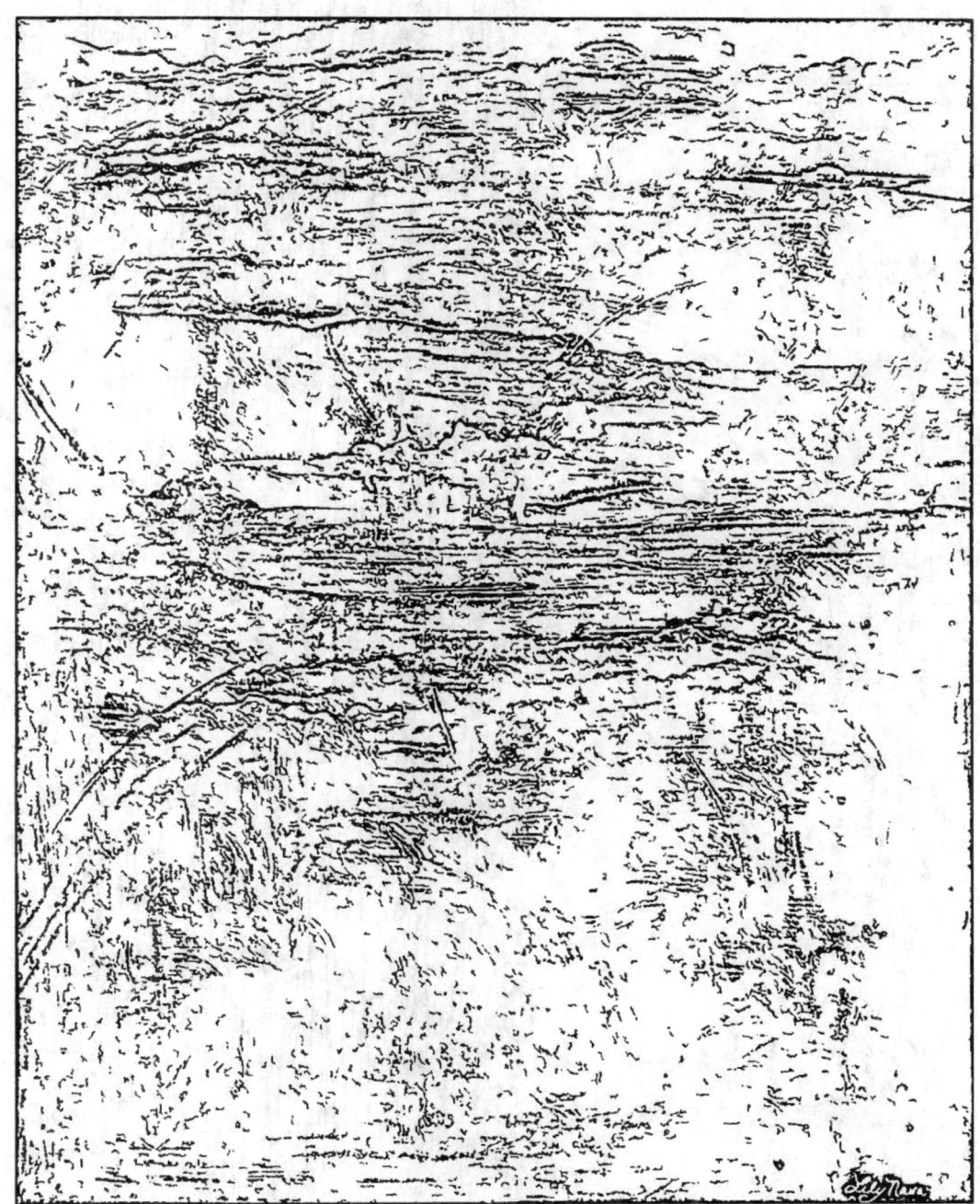

NEW MOON

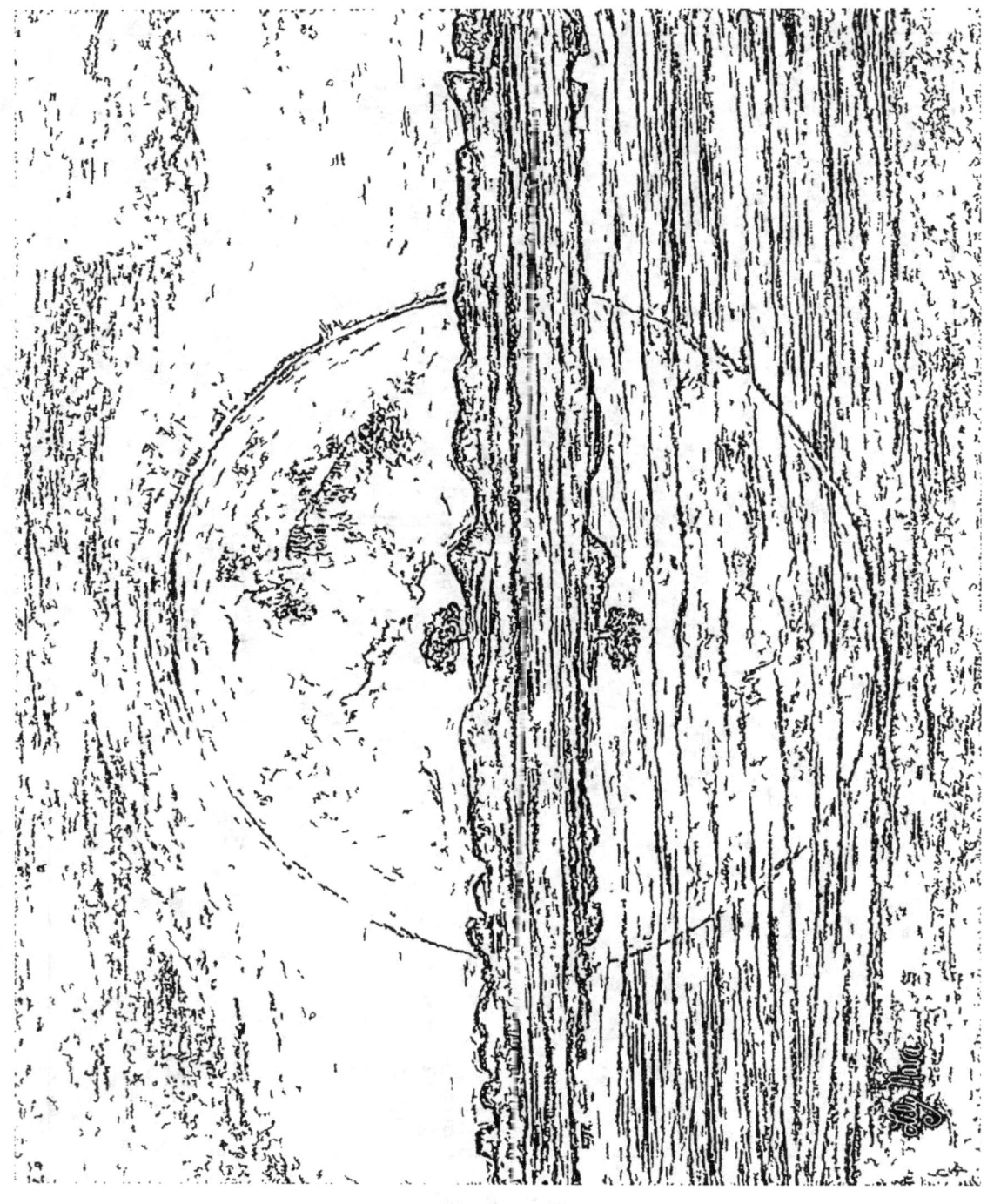

NIRVANA

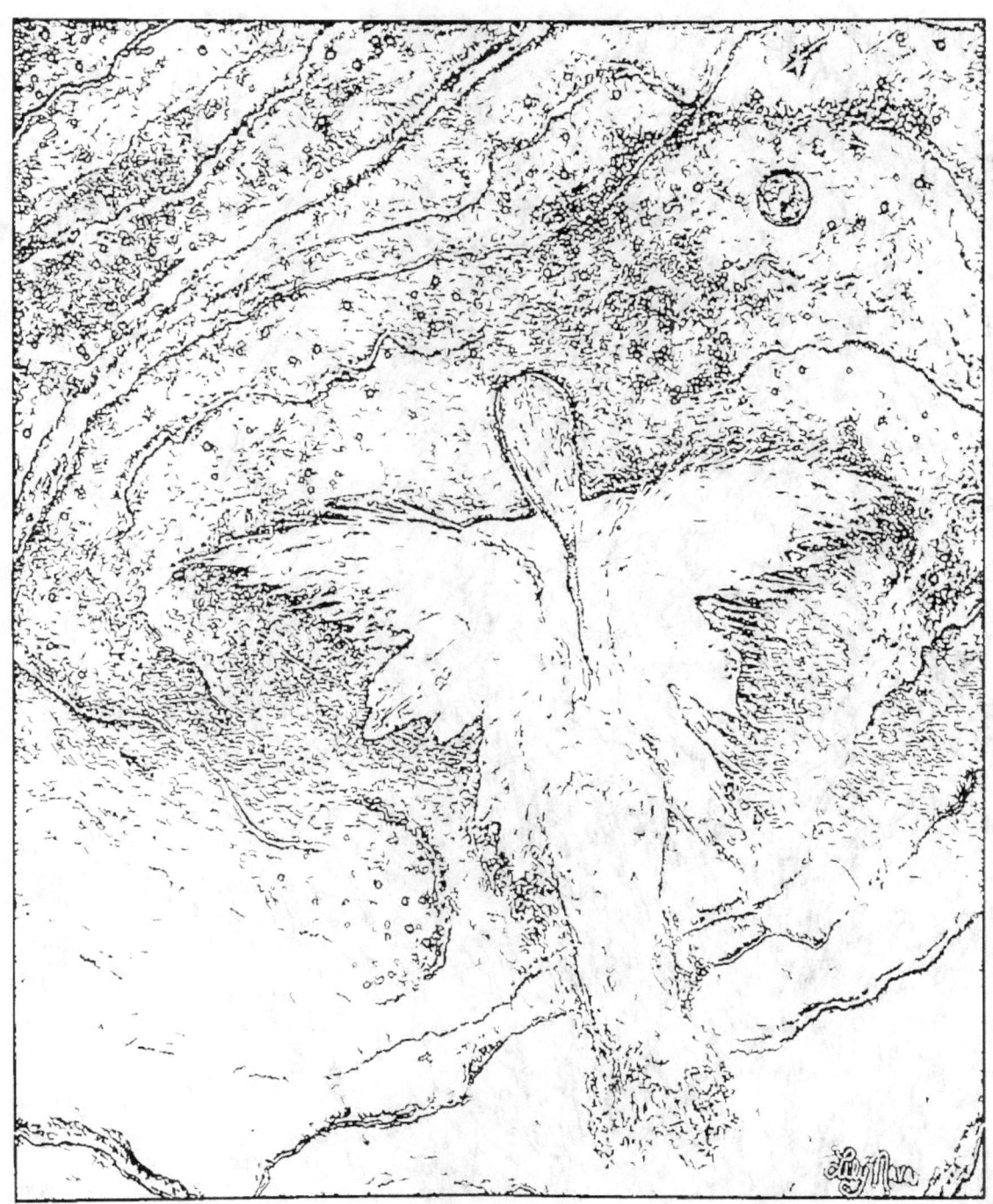
ON CALL

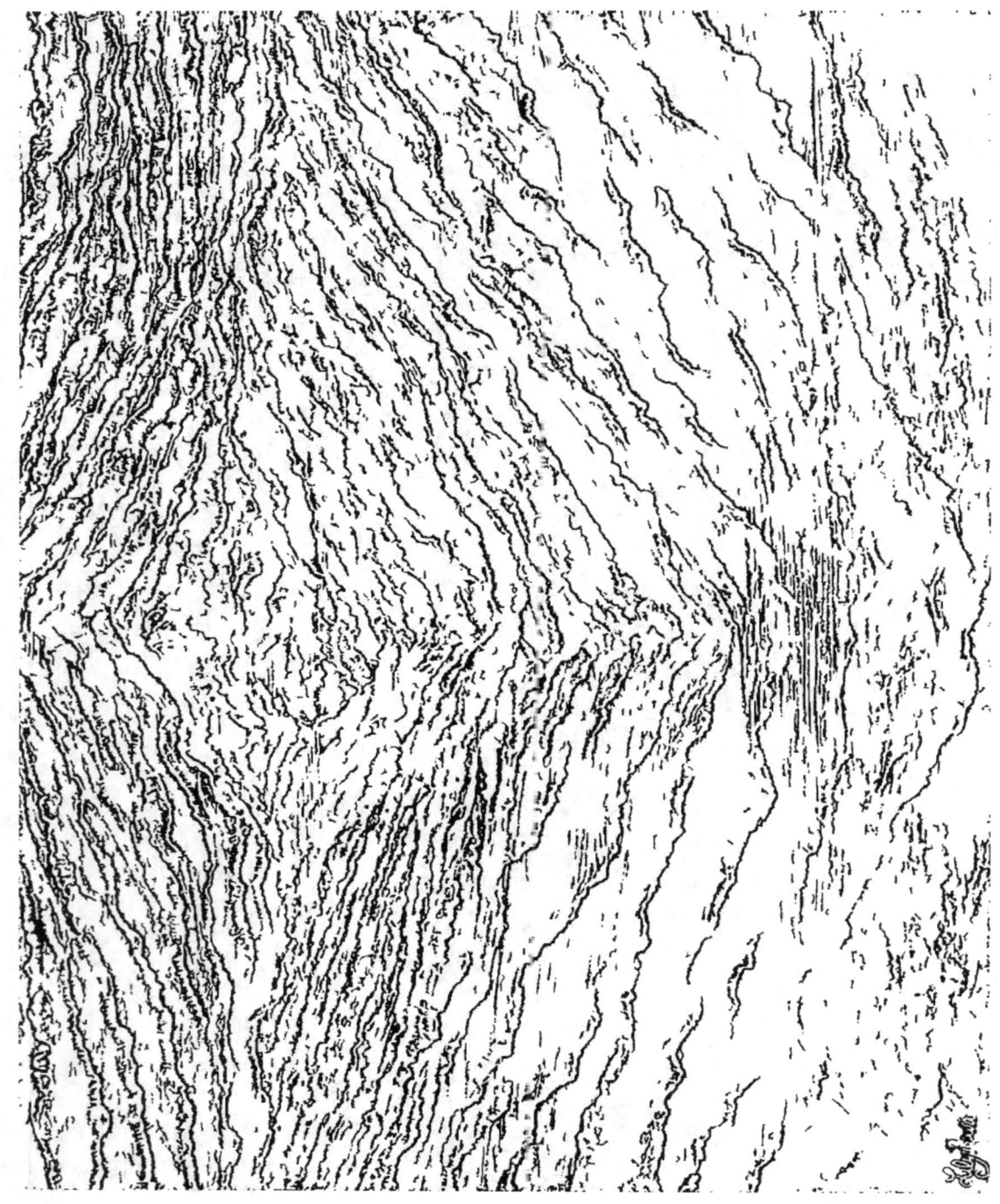

ONENESS

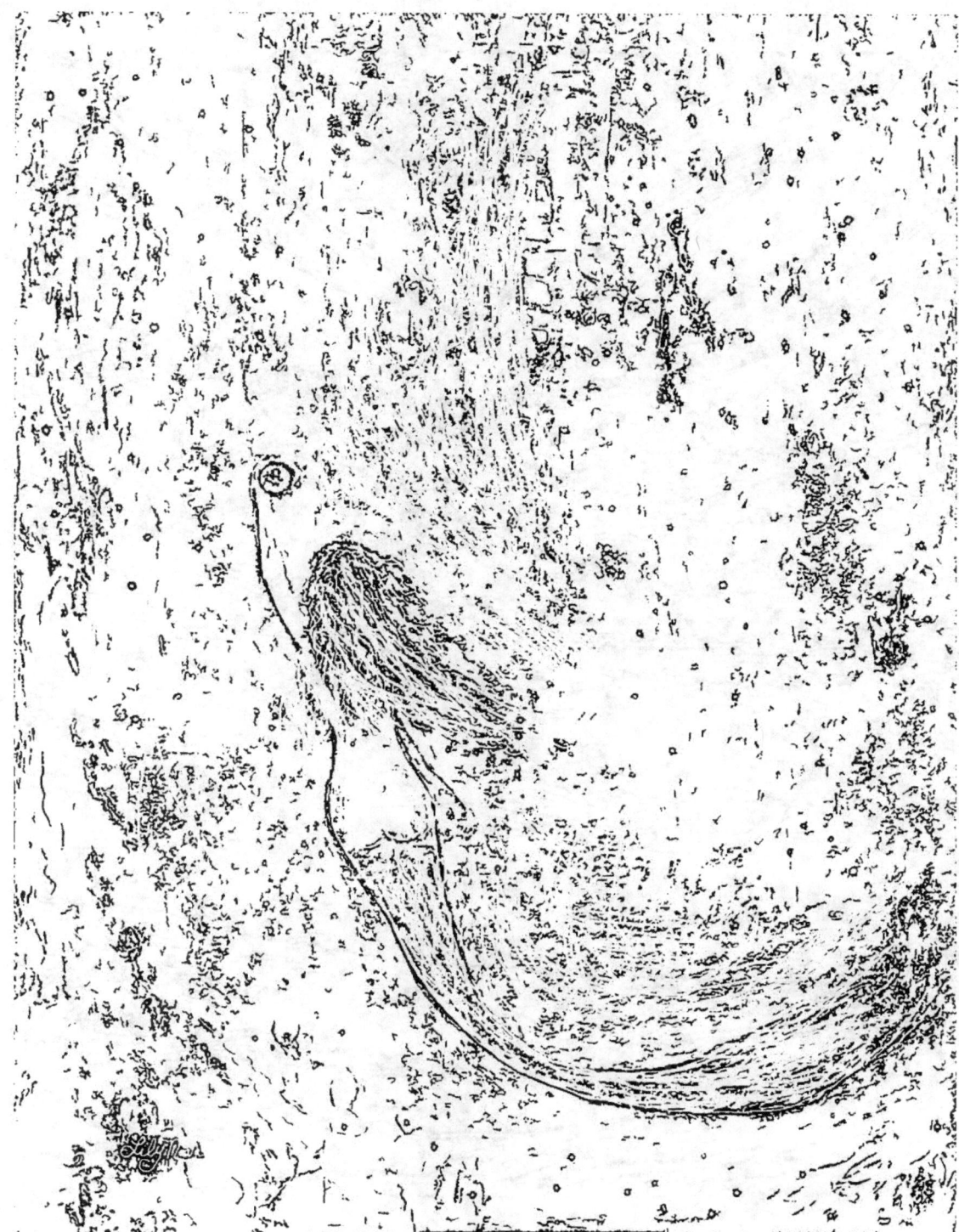

ORACLE

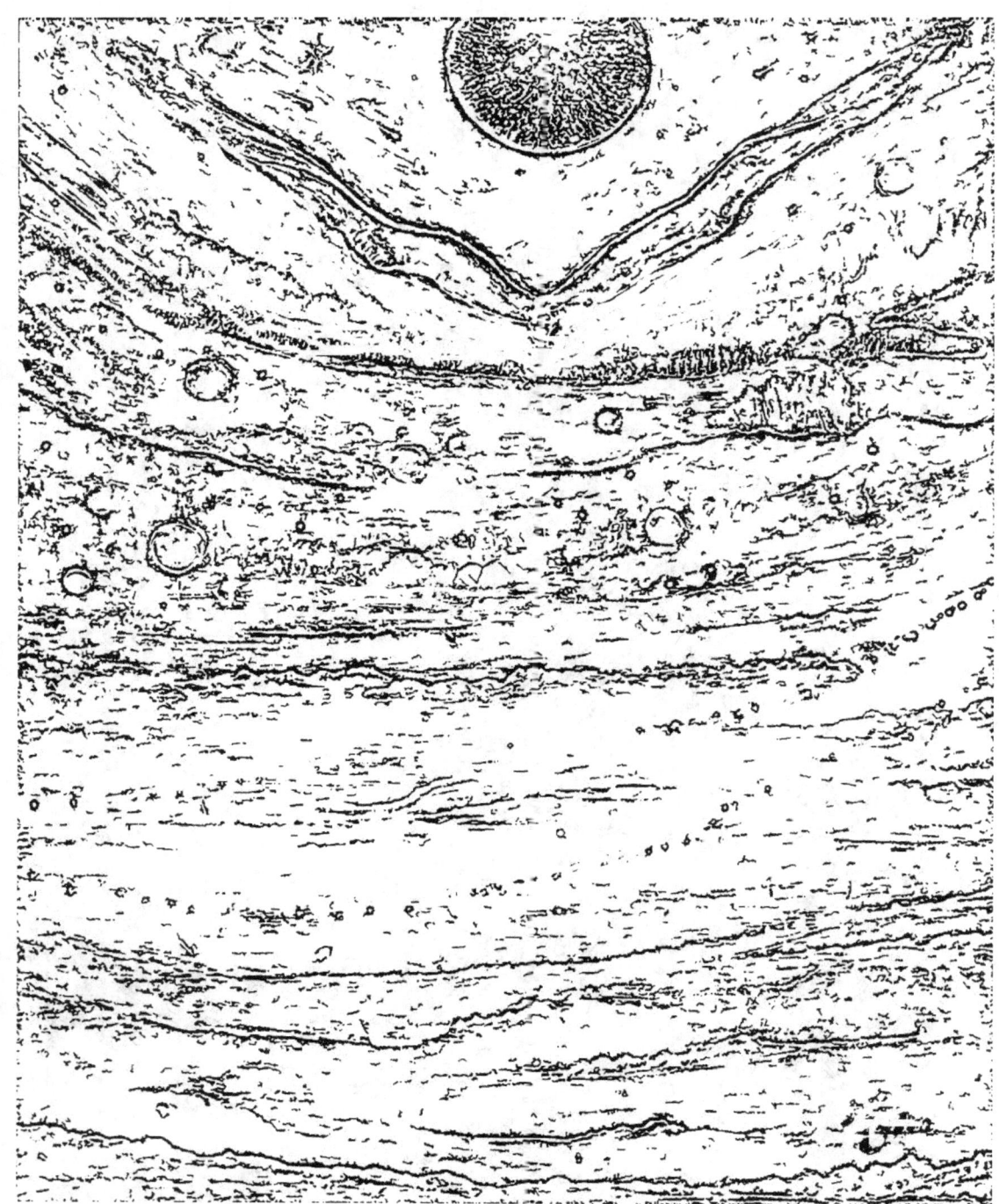

PEACE IS THE WAY

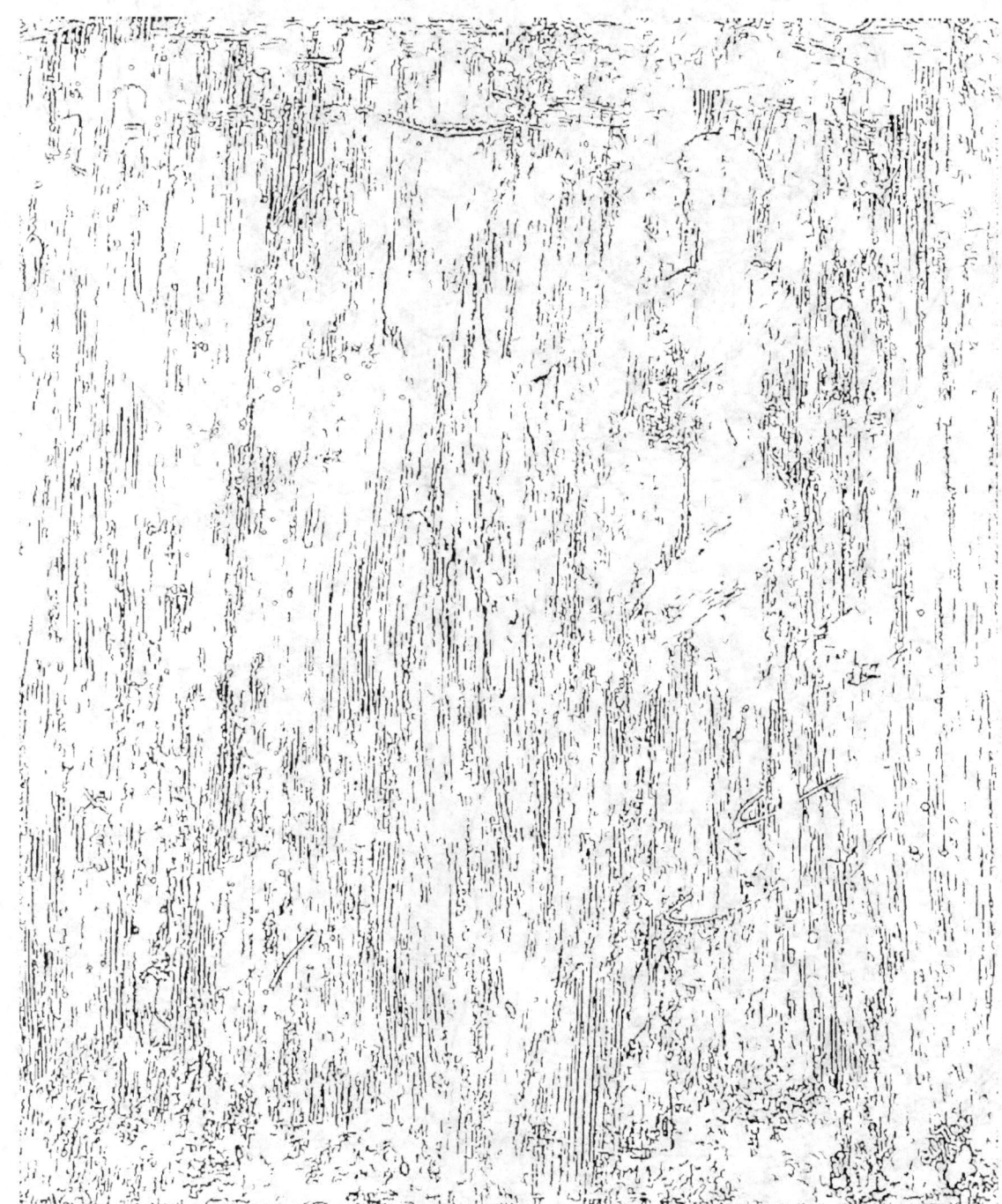

PRISM DANCE

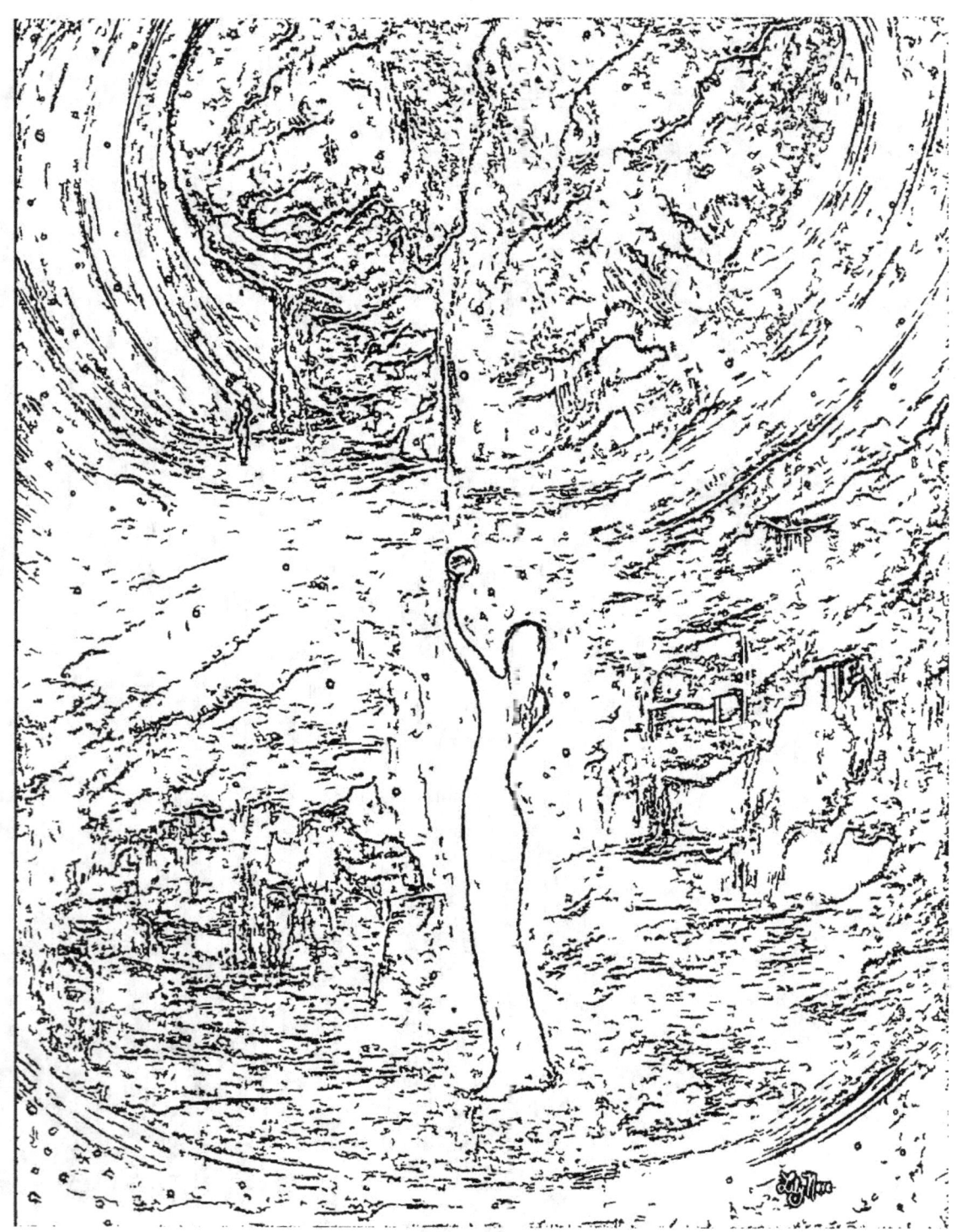
QUANTUM AWAKENING

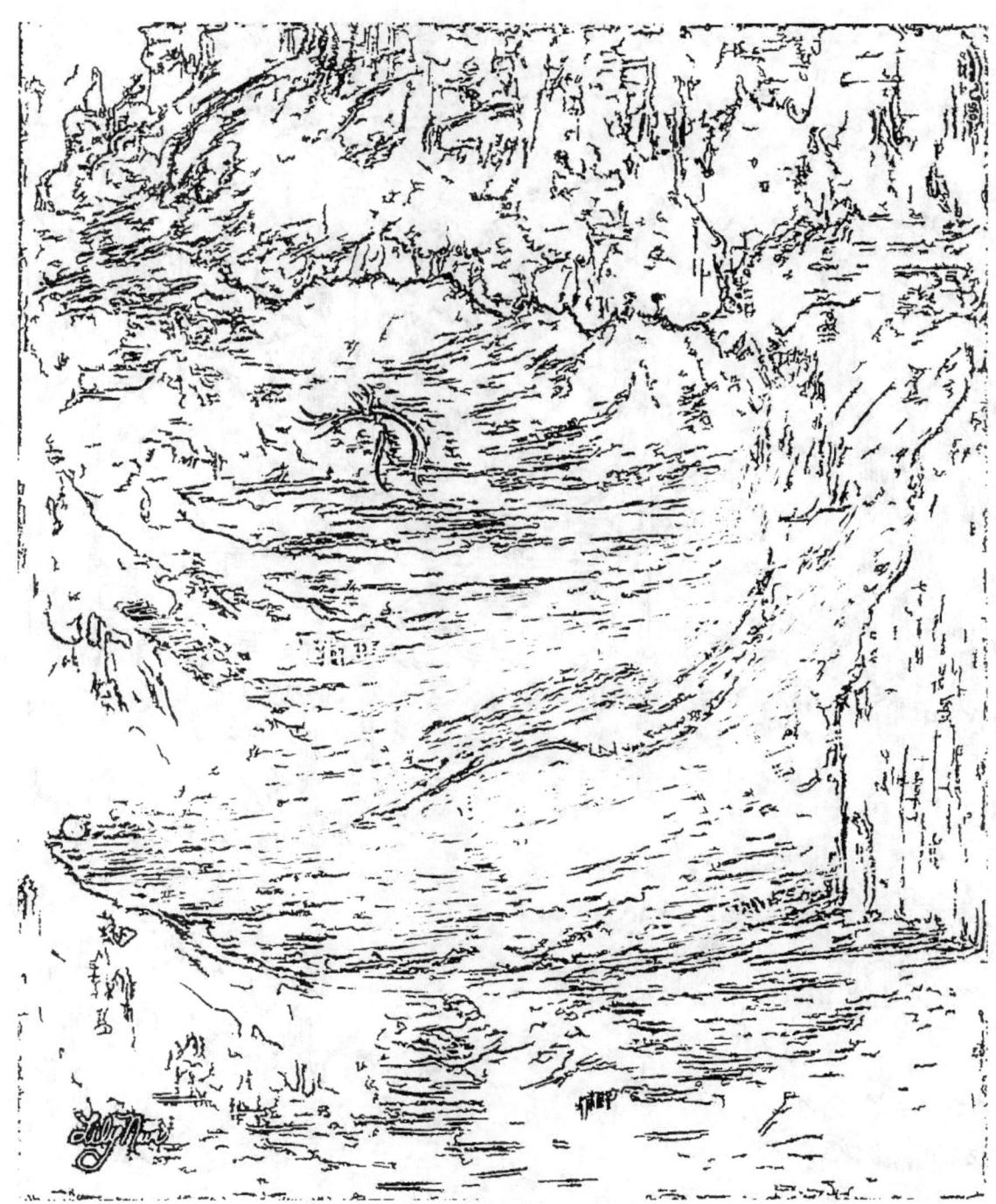

QUEST FOR THE PEARL

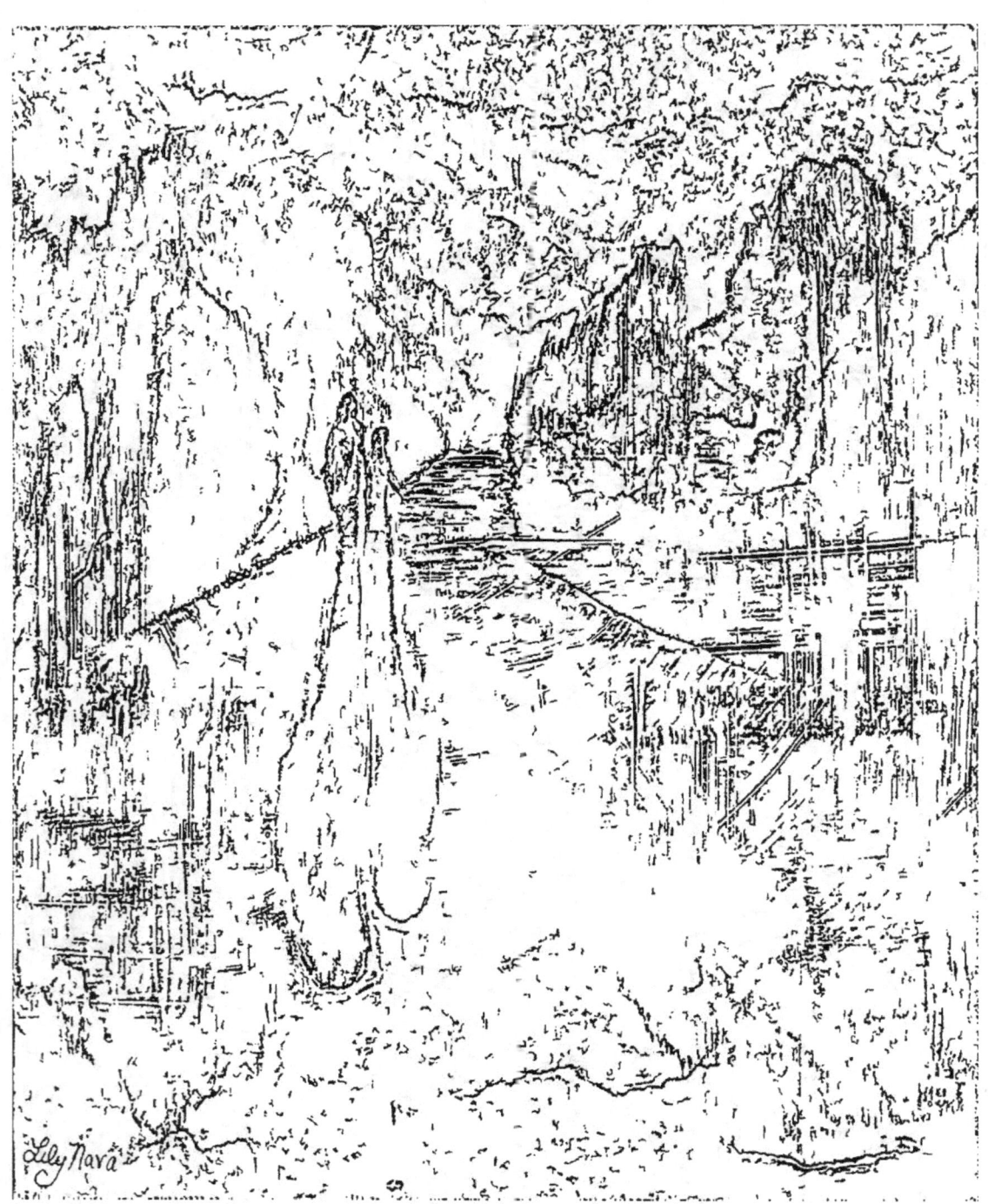

REALITY OF A DREAM

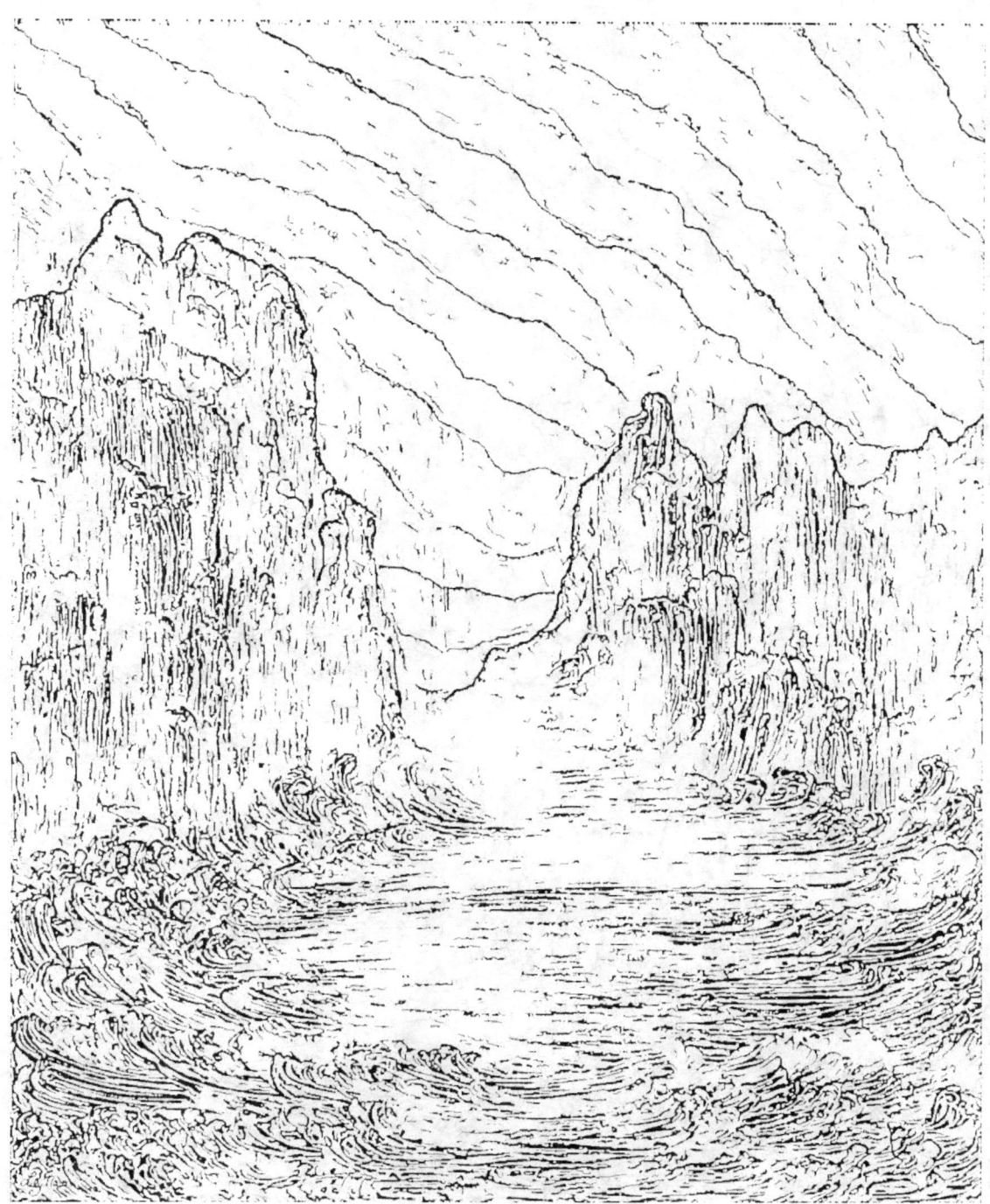

RED ROCK LIGHT I

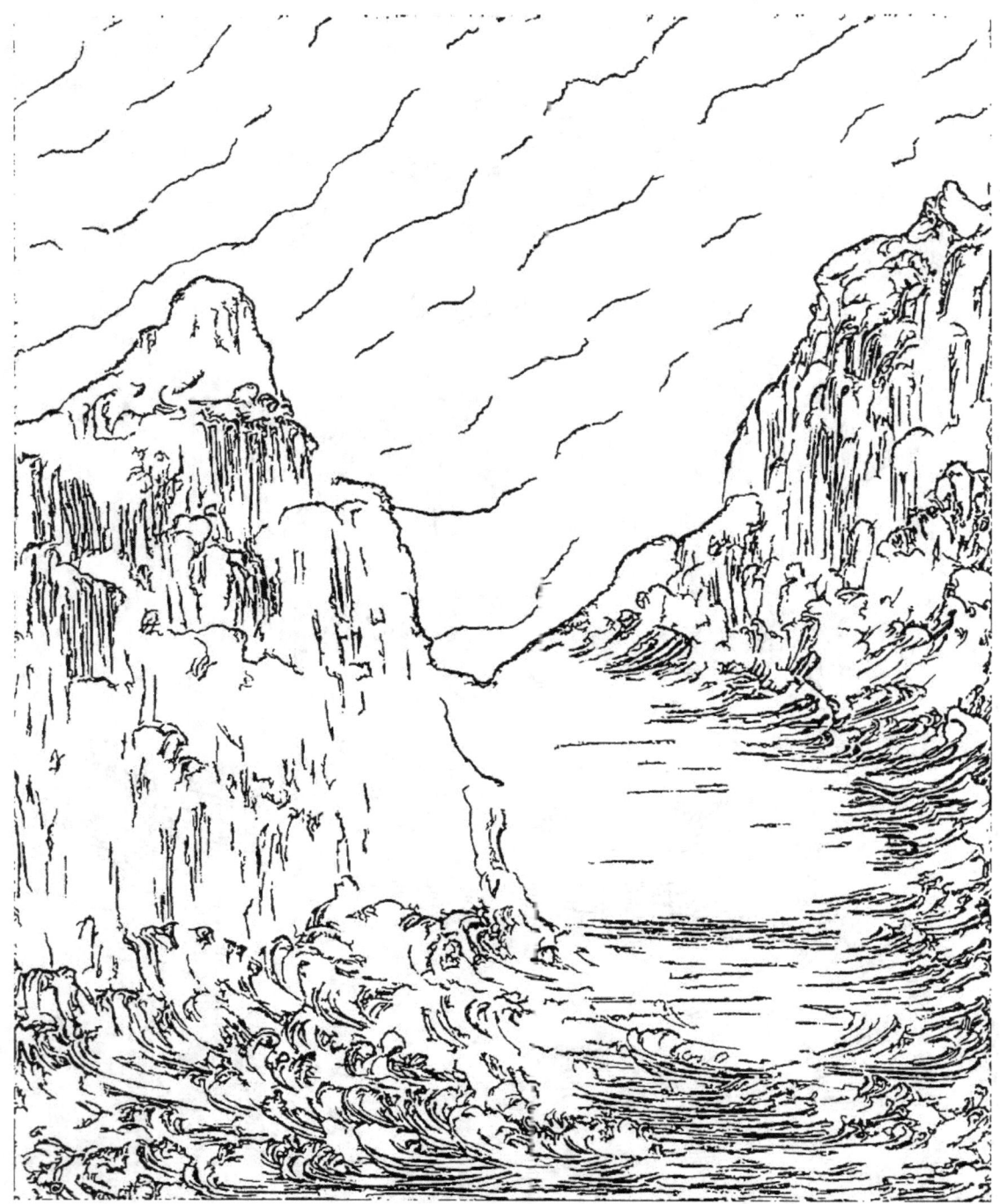

RED ROCK LIGHT II

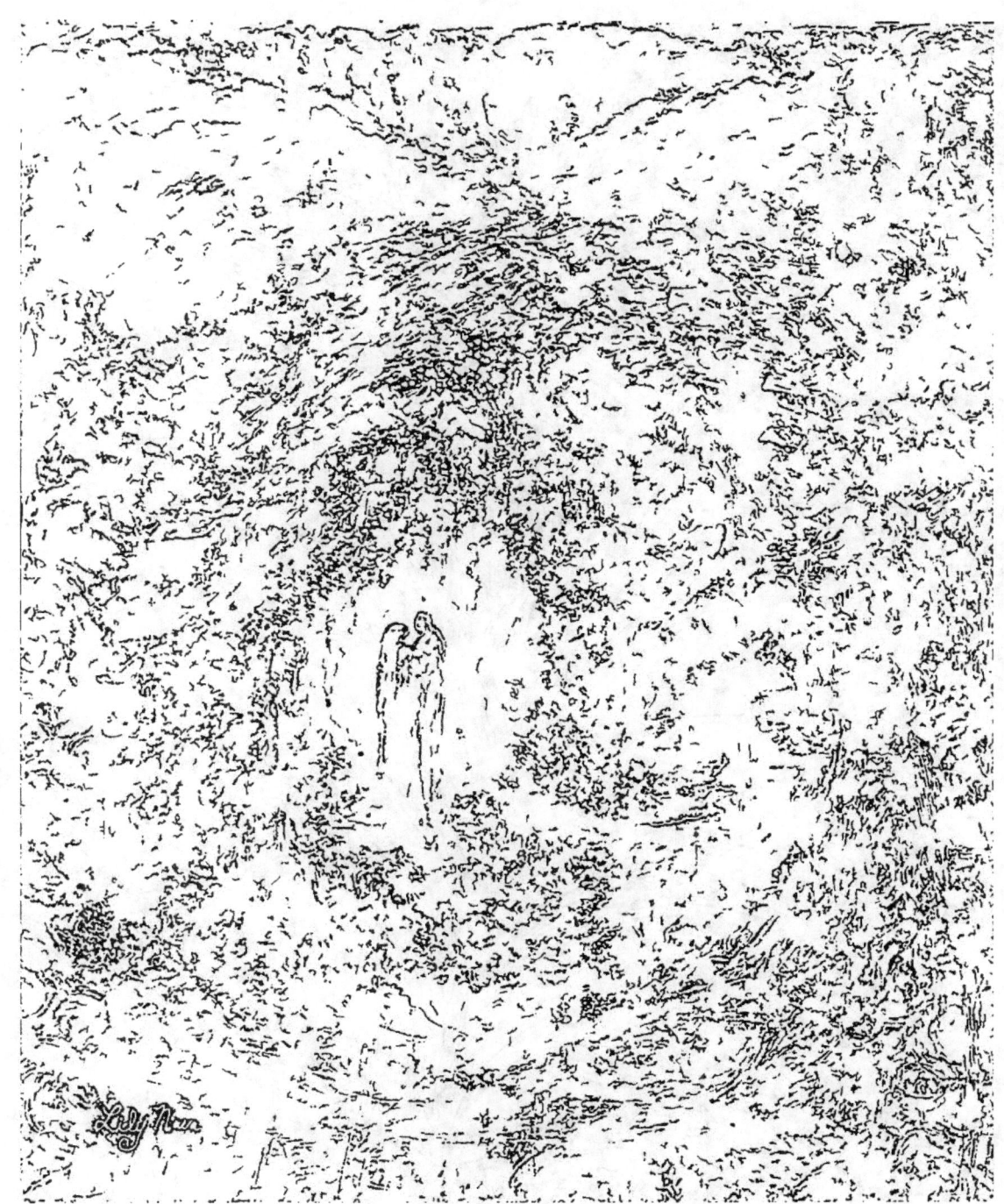

RETURN TO MYSTIC FOREST

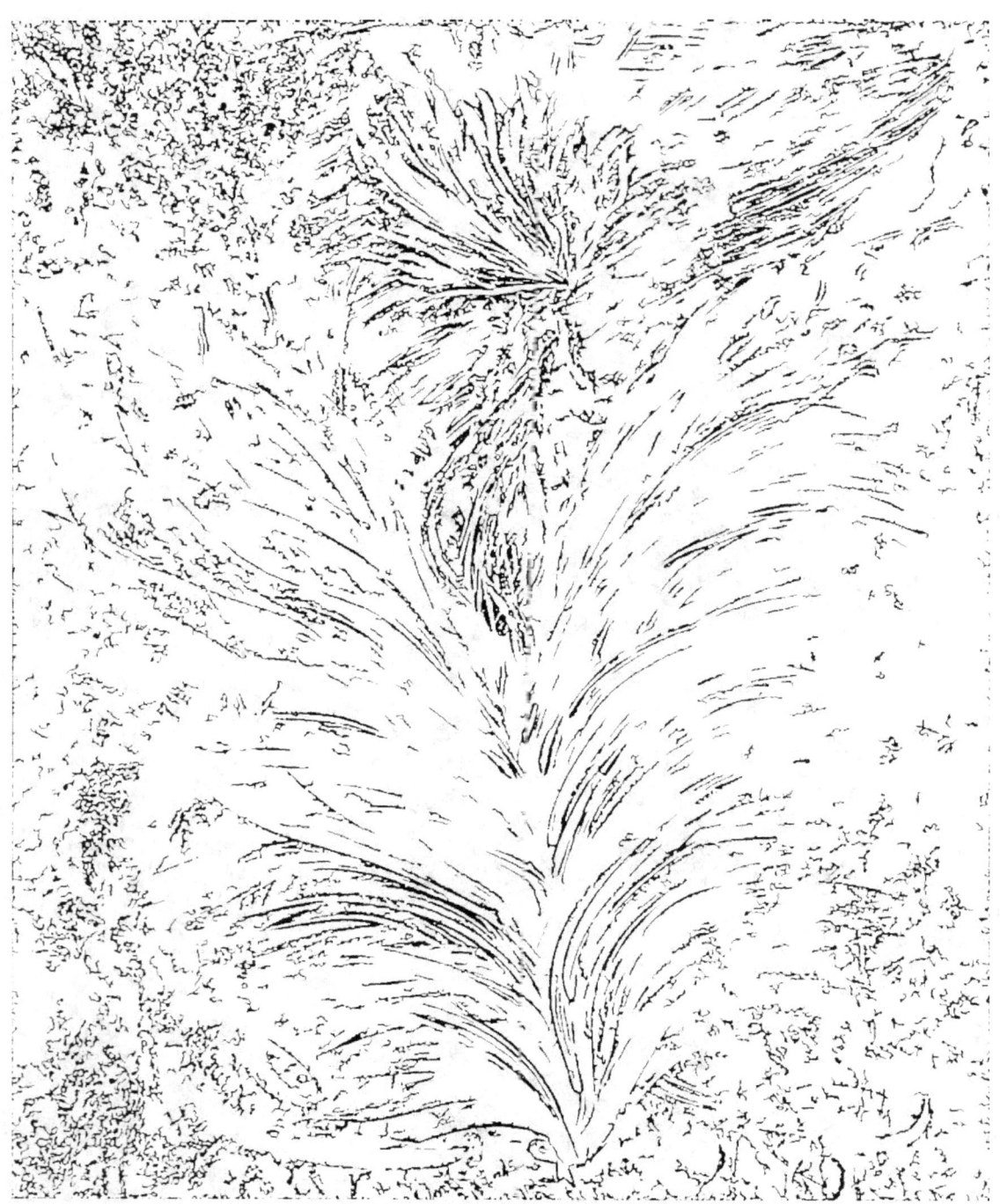

SEA SPIRIT

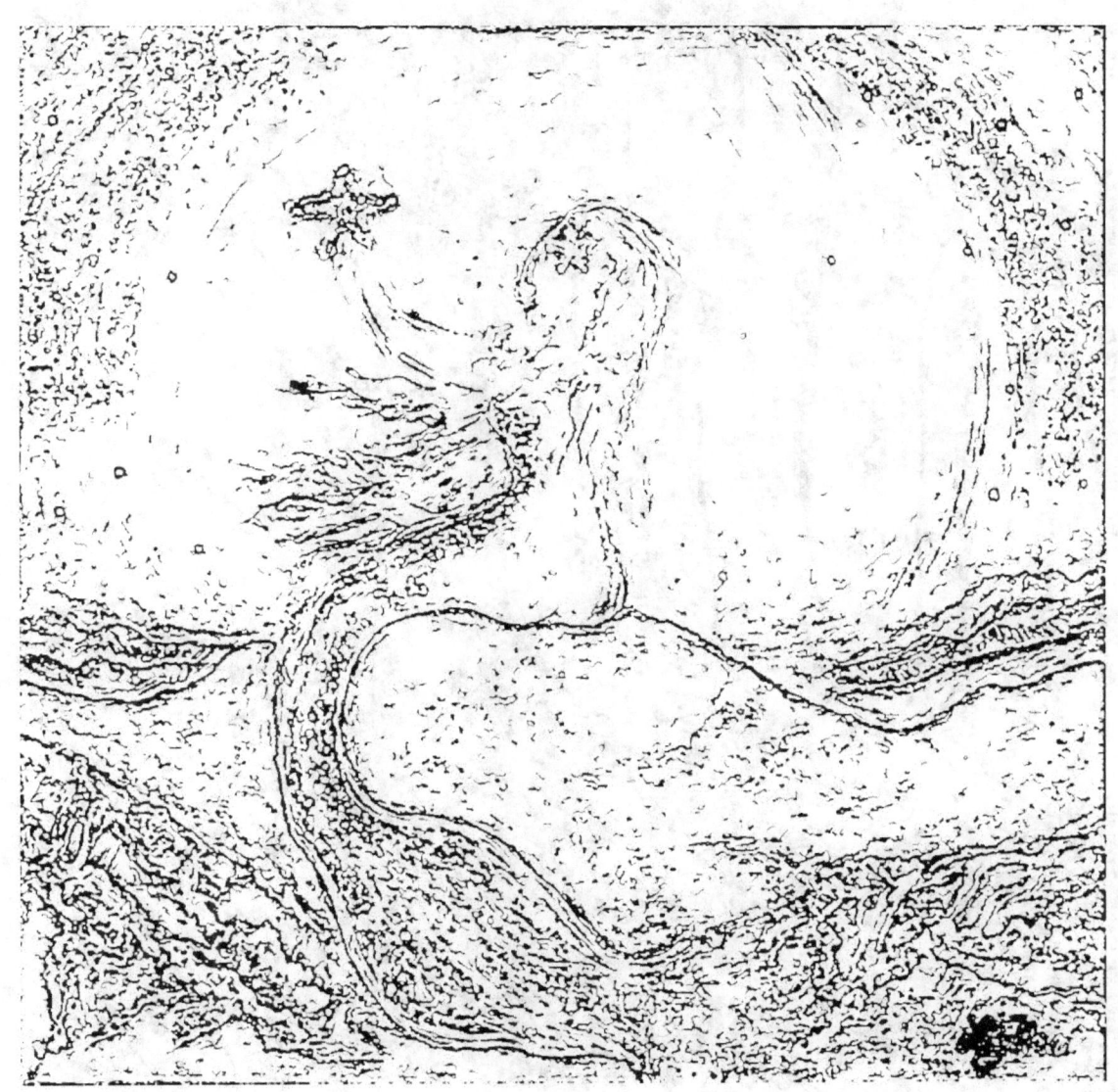

STARFISH

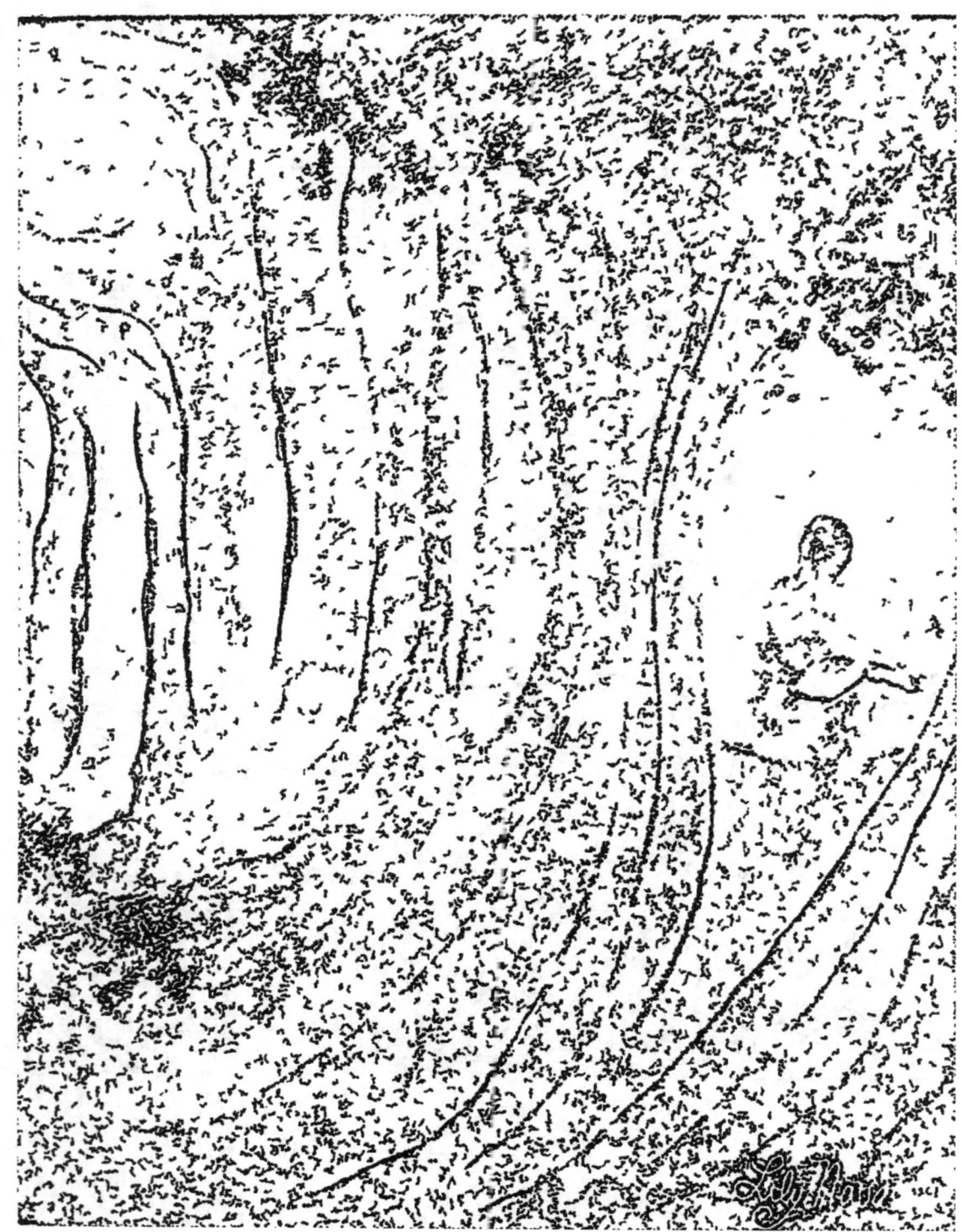

STORYTELLER

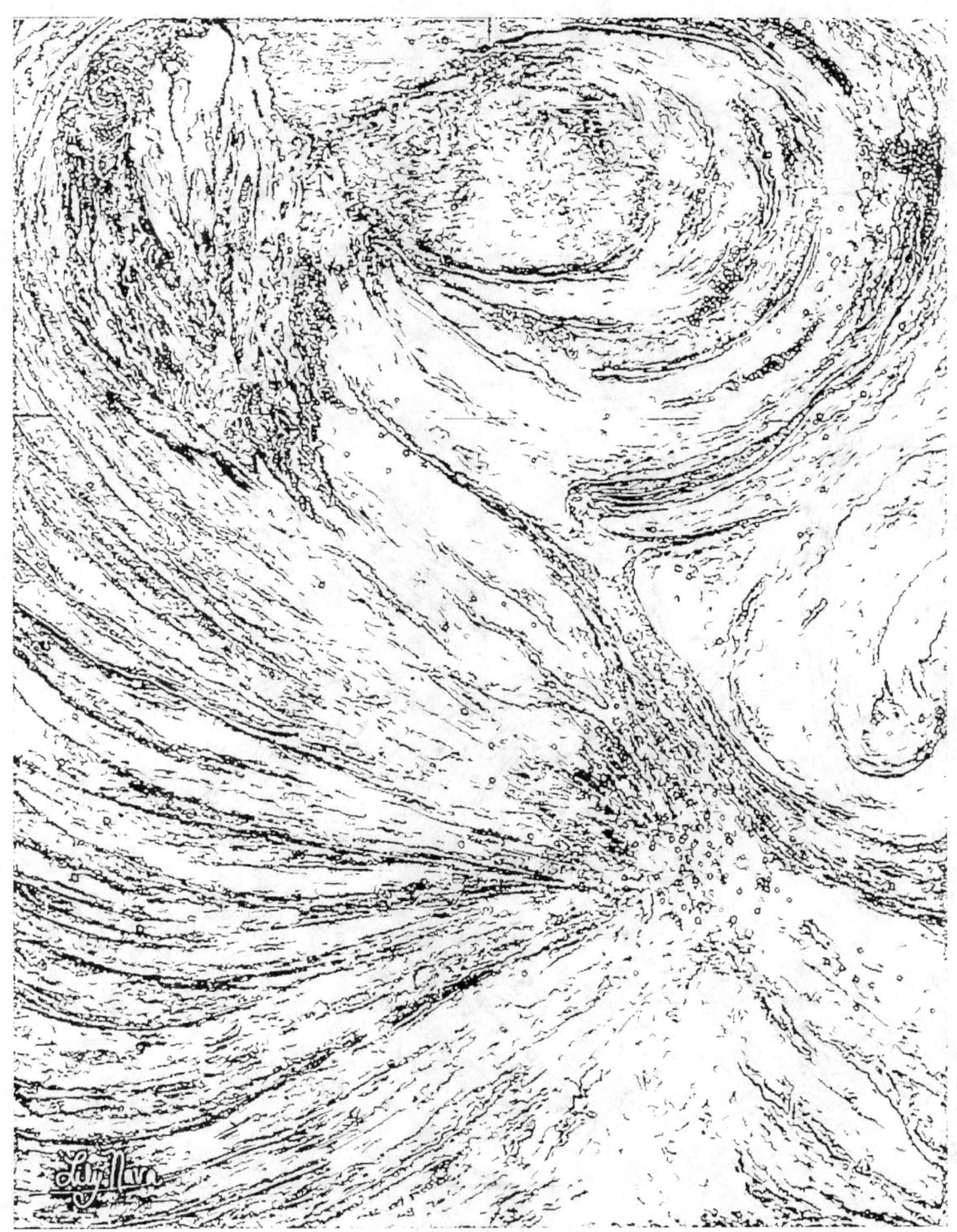

SYNCHRONICITY

TOP OF IMAGE

THE OFFERING

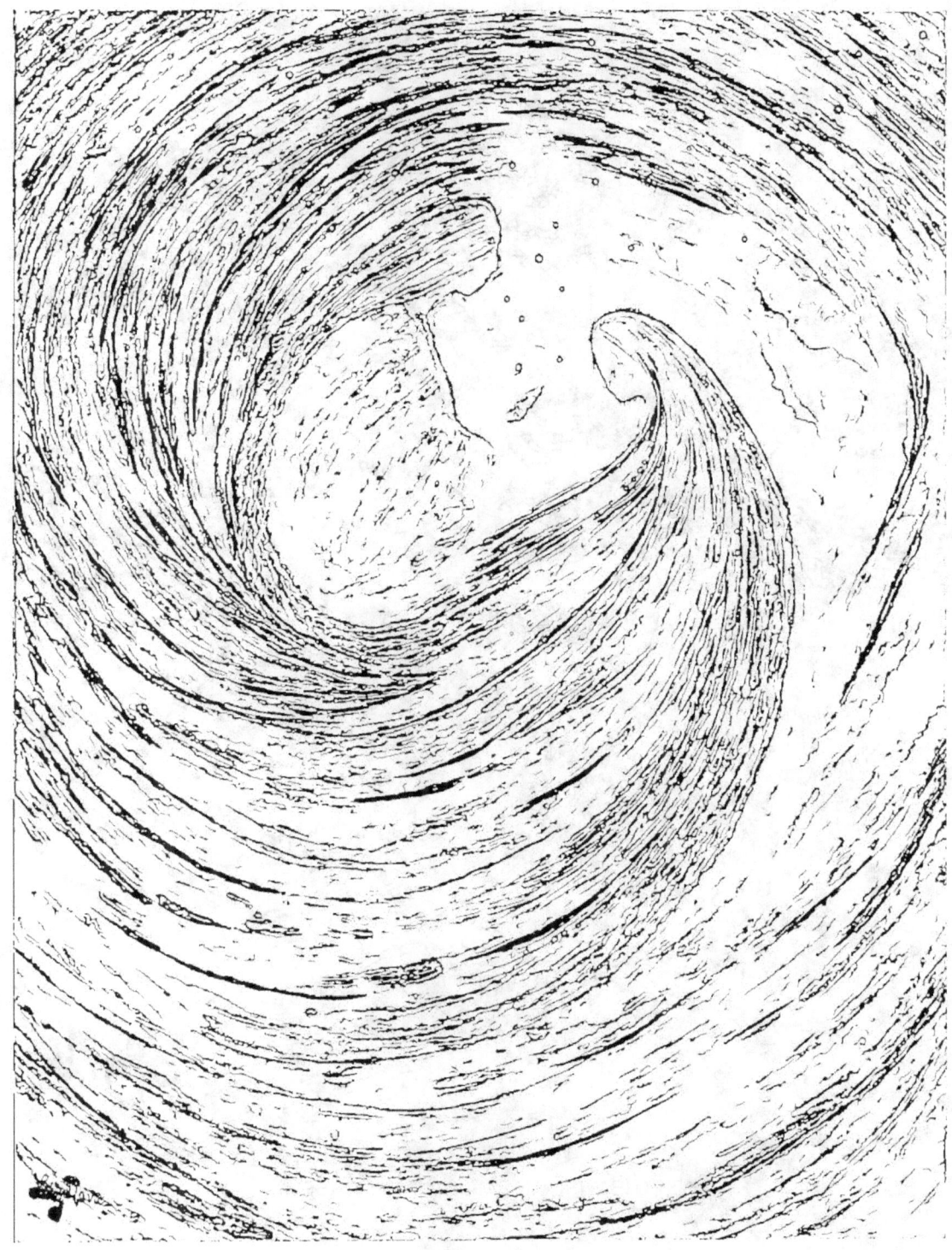

THE SECRET

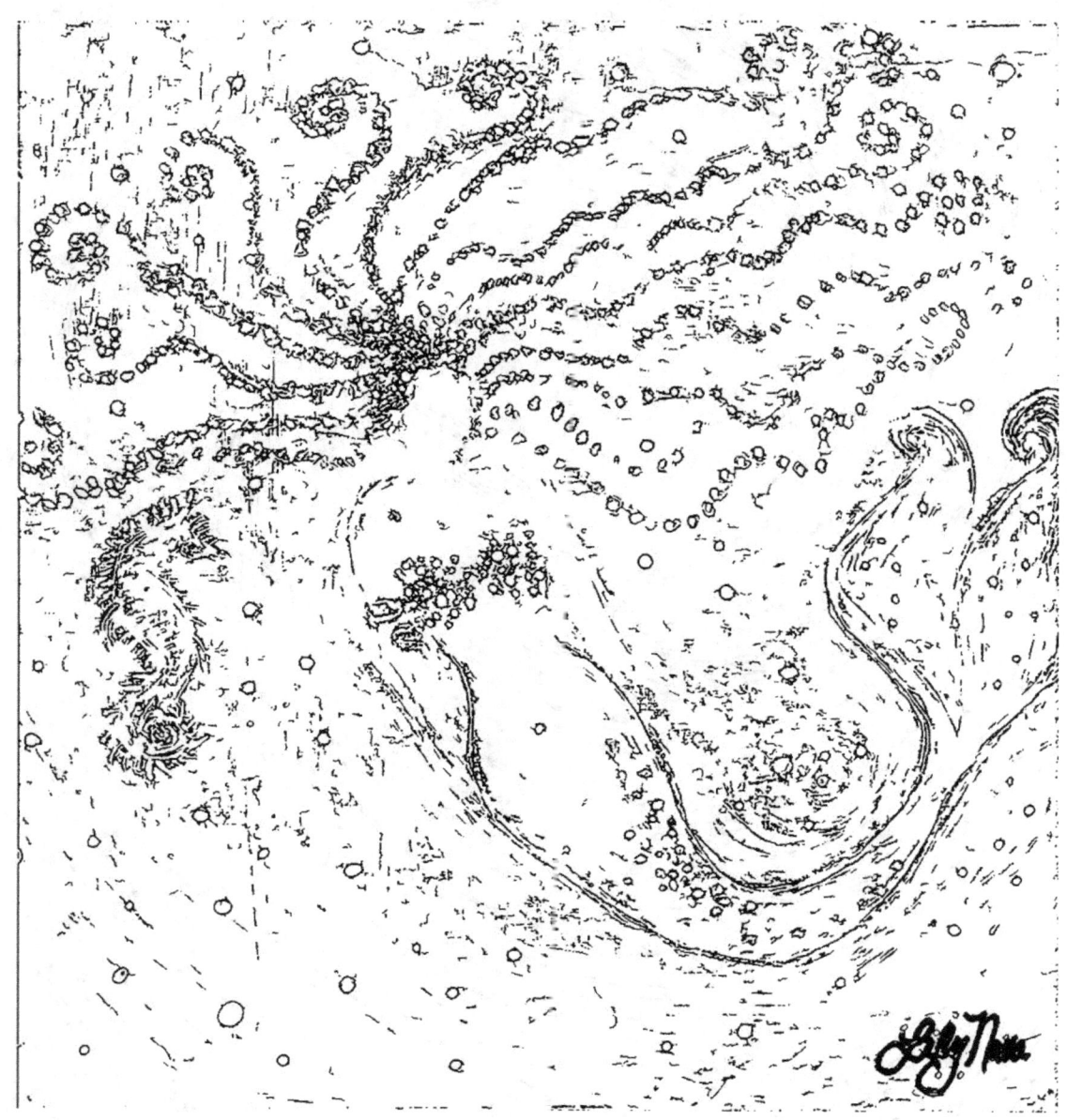

THE WISH-MERMAID & SEAHORSE

TOP OF IMAGE

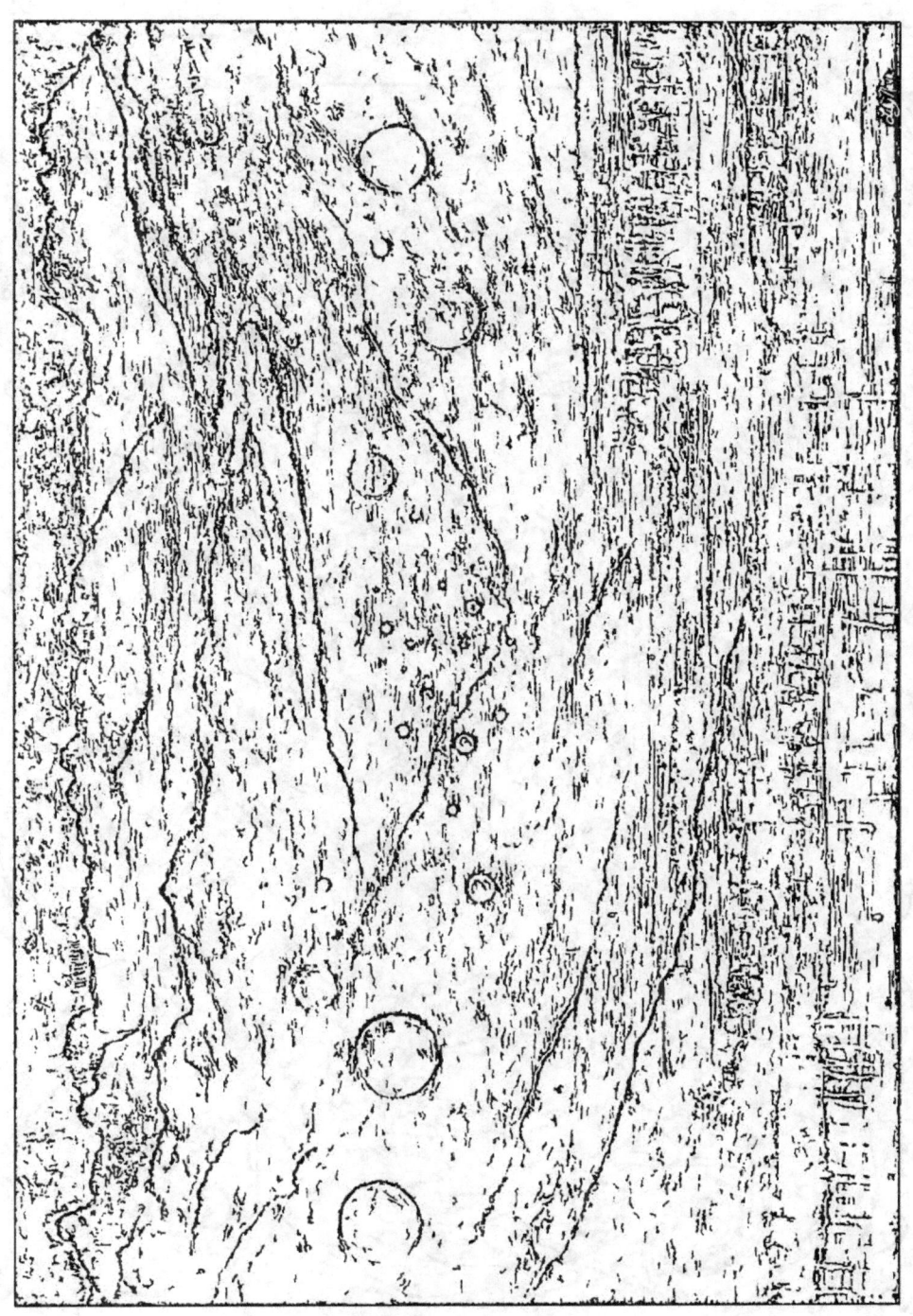

TIMELESS

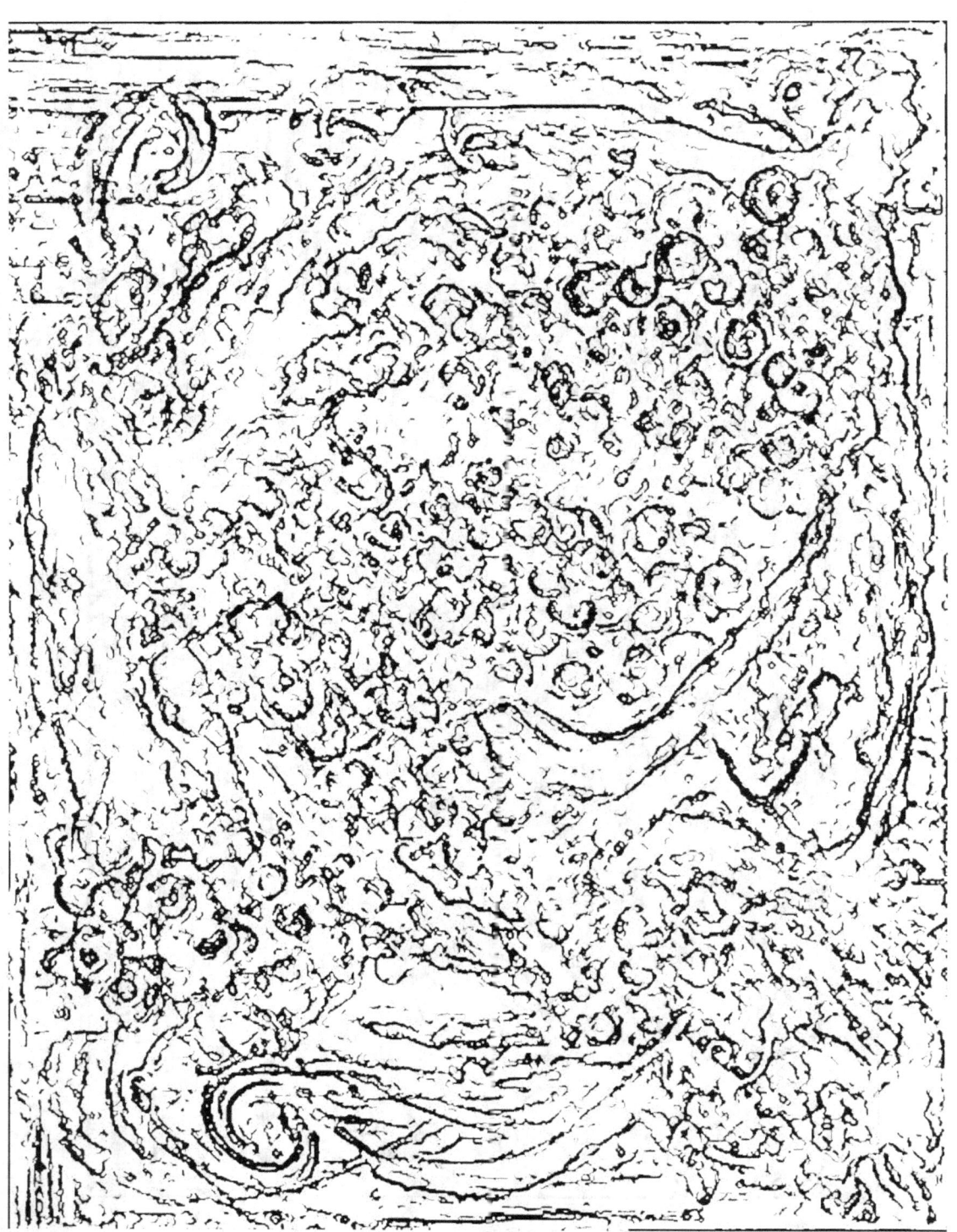

TOP OF IMAGE

TO GAZE WITHIN

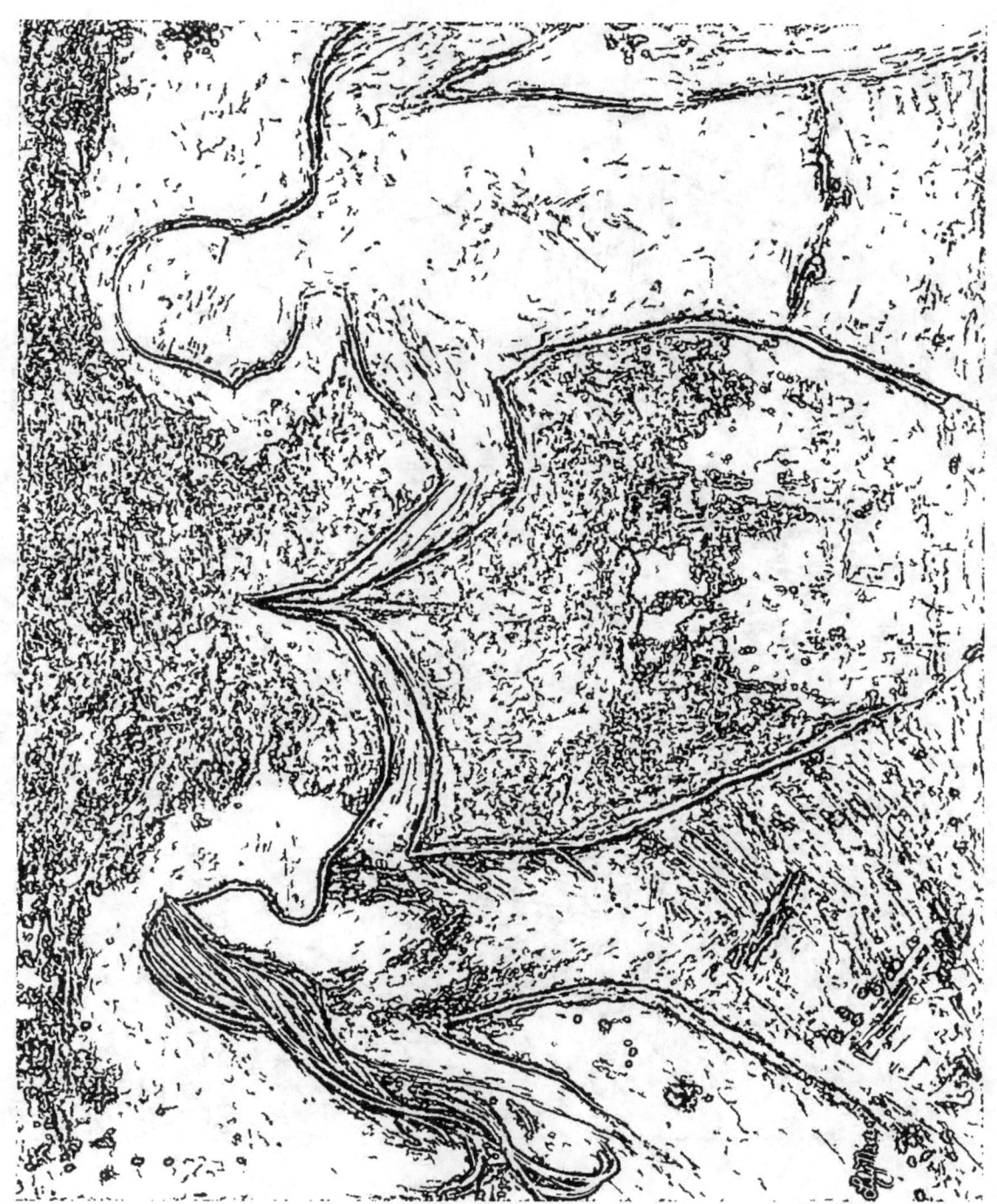

TOUCH

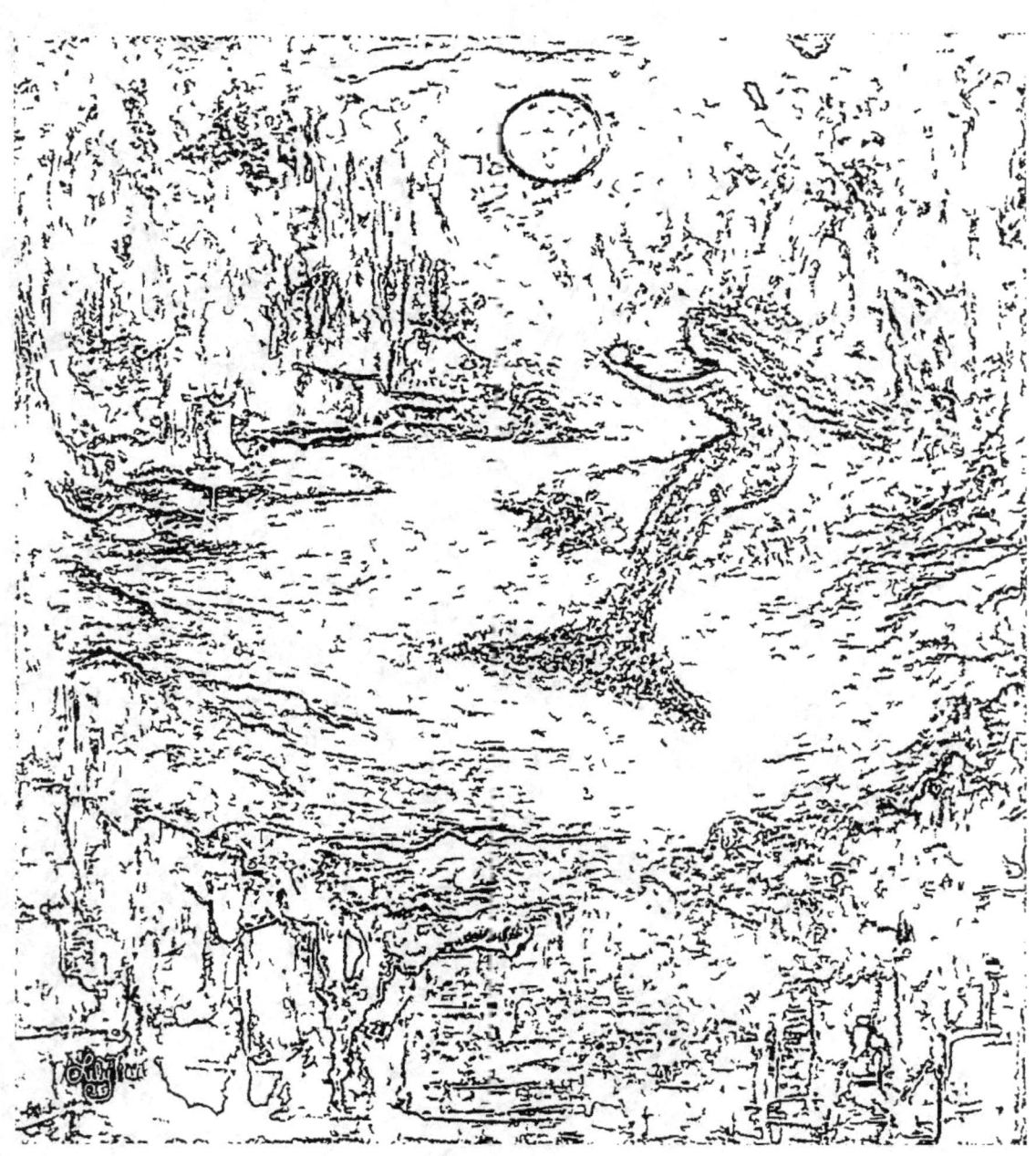

VINTAGE MERMAID-LOVE FOUND

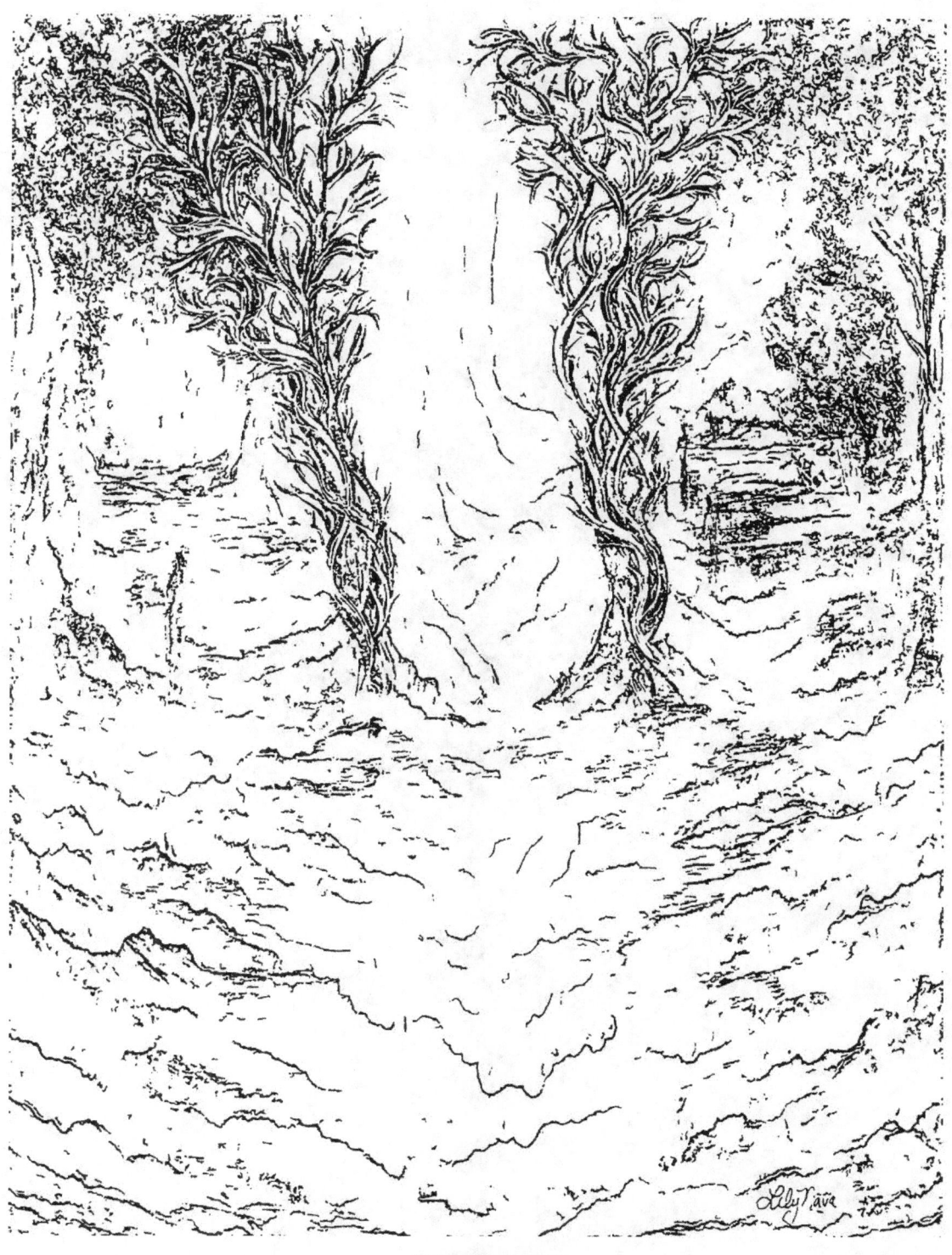

WONDERLAND

www.ingramcontent.com/pod-product-compliance
Lightning Source LLC
Chambersburg PA
CBHW081659220526
45466CB00009B/2813